100% Christianity is the only thi[ng]
inside out. Jago captures the p[ower]
the Gospel offers as well as the [...]
everything. Reading *100% Christianity* leaves y[ou]
conviction that Jago not only believes this, he has experienced [...]
power of Christ's grace and having experienced it, his passion is to
see others capture the 'bigness' of what Christianity actually means.
The greatest challenge is this – Jago reminds us that God has given
us 100% and now God asks us for 100% of our lives. This book hits
the ball into our court, what we do with God's glorious grace and the
message of the cross is the big question we must each answer.
*Malcolm Duncan, Pastor of Goldhill Baptist Church and Chair of Spring
Harvest Planning Group*

100% Christianity deals with some of the key struggles and
challenges in the Christian life, looking at assurance, sin, satisfaction,
evangelism and more. It is rooted in Scripture, written with passion
and humour, and filled with practical applications. Written in a very
readable style, Jago Wynne carefully points us back to the deep
truths of the gospel, and helps to equip us to live all of life for Christ.
John Glen MP, Member of Parliament for Salisbury

Christians are called to commit all they know of themselves to
everything they discover of Jesus Christ. And that's hard work at
times – it stretches our spiritual, mental and physical capacity to the
limits. In this challenging book, Jago calls you and me to shape up
personally to 100% commitment to Jesus as Lord and King. There's
plenty inside for your personal workout, but the questions at the
end of the chapters ask something equally important – can we fold
other people's experiences of the Father into our own and let the
Father create something richer? Jago has done new and not-so-new
Christians a great service here, challenging us all to respond to the
Father's call in Jesus to 'Follow me'.
Canon David Isherwood, Rector of Clapham

It will be near impossible to read this book and not find yourself
bowled over again by the incredible good news of the gospel.
Jago's passion for and presentation of the truth will leave you
challenged and newly inspired, regardless of where you find
yourself in your faith.
Henrietta Metters, Curate, Holy Trinity Brompton

I'm delighted to commend this book by Jago Wynne for two reasons. Firstly, it makes the letter to the Romans accessible, when so often people find it is not. And secondly, it shows why we need the whole letter to live biblically-balanced lives. I think it's a huge help to Christians and non-Christians alike in terms of commentating on what the Christian life is really like.

Rico Tice, Associate Minister at All Souls Church and co-author of Christianity Explored

For Daisy and Boaz and Hope – with 100% love

JAGO WYNNE

100% CHRISTIANITY

HOW THE GOSPEL
CHANGES
EVERYTHING

ivp

INTER-VARSITY PRESS
Norton Street, Nottingham NG7 3HR, England
Email: ivp@ivpbooks.com
Website: www.ivpbooks.com

First published 2014

British Library Cataloguing in Publication Data
A catalogue record for this book is available from the British Library.

ISBN: 978–1–78359–119–0

Set in Dante 12/15pt
Typeset in Great Britain by CRB Associates, Potterhanworth, Lincolnshire
Printed in Great Britain by Ashford Colour Press Ltd, Gosport, Hampshire

*Inter-Varsity Press publishes Christian books that are true to the Bible and that
communicate the gospel, develop discipleship and strengthen the church for its mission
in the world.*

*Inter-Varsity Press is closely linked with the Universities and Colleges Christian
Fellowship, a student movement connecting Christian Unions in universities and colleges
throughout Great Britain, and a member movement of the International Fellowship of
Evangelical Students. Website: www.uccf.org.uk*

CONTENTS

FOREWORD

By Nicky Gumbel

I have this sense of urgency deep down within me. I don't know whether it's because I am getting older or because I am an impatient person. However, I hope it has something to do with the urgency of the New Testament. All Christians believe in the gospel – that's what it means to be a Christian. But not all Christians believe in the urgency of the gospel. The gospel of Jesus Christ is the hope for the world and it is our urgent priority to proclaim it and live our lives in the light of it. As Paul declares, the gospel is 'the power of God for the salvation of everyone who believes' (Romans 1:16).

I recognise that same sense of urgency in Jago – he has an urgent passion for Jesus, an urgent passion for Christians to apply Scripture to their day-to-day lives, and perhaps, particularly, an urgent passion for there to be a real integration in God's people between their heads and their hearts and between their beliefs and their actions.

Jago has a passion for Jesus grounded in much theological study and prayer. He is an outstanding speaker with a great mind (which has brought him impressive academic honours) and it was a huge pleasure to have him and Susannah and their family here with us at HTB for two years.

During that time he was kind enough to devote long hours to helping me with a number of writing projects and his help and advice were invaluable. Even when we took slightly different views on various subjects, his views were always carefully considered and challenging – and he exhibited unfailing grace in hearing my thoughts.

I am delighted that he has written this book and wish it every possible success.

Nicky Gumbel
Vicar of HTB and Pioneer of the Alpha Course

FOREWORD

By Hugh Palmer

Men are often accused of 'compartmentalising' and shutting away some important life factor so that it doesn't affect the rest of their lives. It is not an exclusively male tendency of course and it can have value and advantages but great downsides too.

Both men and women can certainly lock their Christian faith into one or two rooms of their lives so that it does not pervade and affect life in every part. Brains can be engaged but not hearts, as some enjoy the mental wrestling with Christian truths but in a way that never seems to affect their emotions . . . or, just as commonly, vice versa. Or faith will affect our actions in some areas of life but strangely not others.

All the time I have known him Jago has been anxious to integrate Christian faith into life as a whole, to encourage a discipleship that reflects a Christ who is Lord of all and consistently shapes our thinking, feelings and actions. We first met when I joined the staff at All Souls and Jago was leading the ministry to bring Christ to those in the workplace around the church but also teaching and urging the congregation to take their Christian faith to work with them. Now he takes it further integrating faith not just with our working hours but with all of life.

'Present your bodies as a living sacrifice' does not leave exemptions! The New Testament goes further than many evangelists when they call for us to give our hearts to Christ, and many disciples when their faith doesn't stretch further than their head! In this book Jago explores in his usual winsome way all that's involved in a discipleship that takes the apostle's challenge seriously. The advert talks about 'doing just what it says on the tin'. This is a book all about just what it says on the cover, 100% Christianity.

Hugh Palmer
Rector, All Souls Langham Place, London

ACKNOWLEDGMENTS

Thank you to the whole congregation at Holy Trinity Clapham – for your love, encouragement and support, and to many before that at HTB when I first started writing this book, and at All Souls before that when I first preached a series on 100% Christianity from the book of Romans.

Thank you to those many friends who have helped in the production of this book by giving comments on the script or being willing to be used as examples. You are too many to list – but you know who you are! Many true stories have been used in this book, but some names have been changed to protect the identity of the individuals involved.

Thanks to Sam Parkinson at IVP for his invaluable help throughout the whole writing process.

Thank you to my wife Susannah – for her wisdom in life and about life, and her love for me and for our children and for Jesus. Thank you to Daisy, Boaz and Hope – for keeping me real and making me smile.

Thank you to Jesus for his 100% grace: 'Now to him who is able to establish you by my gospel and the proclamation of Jesus Christ . . . so that all nations might believe and obey him – to the only wise God be glory for ever through Jesus Christ! Amen' (Romans 16:25–27).

INTRODUCTION: THE CASE OF THE MISSING 'O'

> I am not ashamed of the gospel, because it is the power of
> God for the salvation of everyone who believes: first for the
> Jew, then for the Gentile.
>
> (Romans 1:16 NIV 1984)

When I was little, I was asked at school to make a giant poster
about my dad, with a description and a portrait. I haven't
included the portrait – I was no budding Van Gogh – but I
hope you enjoy this literary masterpiece:

My daddy
My daddy is quite small and has sticky-up hair.
He likes beans, mince and tomato ketchup.
He likes to play with my leg.
He sleeps a lot because he is quite a sleepy daddy.

If you studied the description of my dad closely, the third
sentence may have left you a little quizzical and confused.
What on earth was my father doing with my leg? Did I have
a wooden leg like a pirate that could be detached and used
as a baseball bat? Did Dad use me as a giant golf club, swinging
me instead of a 9 iron, as he chipped on to the third green?

Was it something more sinister – an initial warning sign for a call to social services?

The truth is that there was a missing 'O' in my ode to my father. Dad actually liked to play with my Leg-o. And, as is so often the case, family traits get passed down the generations, and along with sticky-up hair and a penchant for ketchup and sleeping, I too enjoy playing Lego with my children.

So imagine, if you will, a tower of Lego bricks. A tall tower made up of lots of bricks – all one colour: white. That tower represents you or me or anyone else on this planet. Along comes one red block of Lego which represents the Christian gospel. If we are a Christian, when we heard this Christian gospel we received the red block and welcomed it. We didn't reject it and throw it away, but accepted it positively.

But what did this acceptance of the gospel actually look like? I think that for most of us, it looks like a red block of Lego stuck on top of the tall white tower. Our faith is merely attached to the original us. I'm still the same old me, with a nice Christian bit bolted on top. However, it is an addition that can then be removed, when it is embarrassing or awkward: whenever we're cross or lustful or greedy, whenever life would be easier without it. The red block can be removed whenever there is a cost to being a Christian that we'd rather not bear. I think that is the picture for most of us, most of the time. Certainly for me.

There are at least three ways that this bolt-on Christianity becomes evident:

1. 100% g_spel – the content of the gospel we believe gets changed. Bits get taken out. It's much easier to take off the Christian block if we have first changed its definition. We water down Christ's claim on our life to little more than a lifestyle option, which perks us up

when we feel down. There's a hole – a missing 'O' – in our gospel about Jesus.

2. 100% passi_n – the relevance of the gospel becomes muted. We feel less need to be passionate about it, and, more particularly, less need to be passionate about Jesus. We become more excited about our own achievements, or the achievements of our spouse or children, than we are about Christ's achievements. When people sign off a letter or text, if they're writing to someone they care for greatly, they show their passion for them with an 'O' as well as an 'X'. 'O' stands for a hug. There's a hole – a missing 'O' – in our passion for Jesus.

3. 10_% life – our obedience in response to the gospel becomes sidelined. At the end of Paul's letter to the Romans, he declares that 'your obedience is known to all' (Romans 16:19 NRSV). The same cannot be said for many of us. All too often, we don't let Jesus make a difference in massive sections of our lives outside the time we gather for church on a Sunday. Ours isn't 'whole-life discipleship'. More like 10%-life discipleship. Certainly not 100%. There's a hole – a missing 'O' – in our life with Jesus.

What I describe is a challenge that faces me personally. I am guessing it faces you too. And when we are faced with a challenge, we have two options. We can bury our heads in an 'O' in the ground and pretend the problem doesn't exist. Or we can face up to it. To do that, we need to think through how Jesus and his gospel can no longer just be a bolt-on extra to our lives, but rather influence everything. This book is about how the gospel changes everything.

The Christian call is not just to be a tall white tower with a block of red that can come on or off depending on the circumstances. The call is for you and me to be transformed into a tall *red* tower and let the Christian gospel influence us 100%. The gospel should take root in every area of our lives, in all times and in all places and in all circumstances. It is to impact our mind, our heart and our will. It is to affect our thoughts, our emotions and our actions.

In the past, I have been amazingly privileged to work on the staff of two of the largest Church of England churches in the UK: All Souls, Langham Place and Holy Trinity Brompton (HTB). I was one of the associate ministers at All Souls for five and a half years and then, having been ordained, I was a curate at HTB for two years. Of course, as with any two churches, there are differences. One is more 'conservative', the other more 'charismatic'. One has produced the Christianity Explored course, the other Alpha.[1] Yet, far more importantly, both churches are united in aiming to live out and declare all of the gospel with all passion in all of life.

And yet, of course, neither of these two churches is perfect. Above all, the gospel is not perfectly lived out because both communities are made up of imperfect human beings who sin and are sinned against. It's exactly the same with the church I am now serving in: Holy Trinity Clapham. Whoever we are, whatever church we are or are not a part of, we are all rebels and victims. We are all people who squabble and struggle and suffer, who get depressed and doubt and die. We all have our unique life-situations and challenges and experiences, some of which are positive and others negative. But all of us can look for God to be at work in us by his Spirit, helping us to receive and respond to the 100% gospel with 100% passion in 100% of life.

Much of this book uses Paul's letter to the Romans to address the significant issue of how Jesus has an impact on everything in our lives. (However, this is not a commentary

on Romans; there are plenty of those around to read.)[2] Many
people would say that the verse quoted at the start of this
section gives the theme of the whole letter in a nutshell. Paul
writes, 'I am not ashamed of the gospel, because it is the
power of God for the salvation of everyone who believes'
(Romans 1:16 NIV 1984). The apostle Paul wanted to be a 100%
Christian, never ashamed, but rather living out *all* of the
gospel with *all* passion in *all* of life.

My prayer is that, through the power of the Spirit, this book
may help you joyfully to have the same desire as Paul. Of
course, you and I will still, all too often, fail and sin and
stumble. But I pray that more and more, you will know a
greater desire and a greater freedom to live out that 'red
tower' life where you and the Christian gospel never become
detached from each other.

PART 1: 100% GOSPEL

Despite horrendously potent aftershave, Nigel the driving instructor was a good tutor in all things necessary to pass a driving test. That was, until one fateful day in January, when, just after some heavy English rainfall, Nigel decided to get me to drive through a local ford to 'test my clutch control'. I drove down the hill, but brought the car to a halt in front of the ford to survey the water flowing across the road. It looked significantly deeper than normal. I asked whether he really wanted me to try to drive through this torrent, but Nigel insisted that this would be a useful thing for me to do. So forwards I went, with the water getting deeper and deeper until it rose up to the handles on the car doors.

At this point Nigel began to fear that it might have been a bad decision to send us into the ford, and so, using the dual foot controls of a driving instructor's car, he tried to put the car in reverse and drive it back out. It was too late. The car had started floating, and moments later water started pouring in. Thankfully, this was in the era before electronic windows, and so we wound down our windows, climbed out, and sat on the roof of the car before jumping into the river to go and search for help.

While I was delighted by the unique and entertaining experience of my lesson, Nigel was mortified. His car had to be towed out of the ford, and was written off. All the other driving instructors he worked with heard about what had happened. In the central office, on the sign that stated his name and his job title – Driving Instructor – colleagues regularly scratched out the 'r' in 'driving' to turn Nigel into an expert in tuition of a more aquatic nature.

A seemingly small difference – just one letter – actually produces a very big difference. I doubt Nigel would have been a great success as a Diving Instructor. When it comes to the gospel, it is just the same. A seemingly small difference in what is proclaimed can actually produce a very big difference.

There are those who proclaim a gospel that is less than 100%, with some small element scratched out. This might be a gospel with no mention of the plight all humans naturally face, or the cost of being a Christian, or the empowering presence of the Holy Spirit, or the fact that the gospel is not just about a personal ticket to heaven, but about Jesus as Lord over all creation and all of life.

Others proclaim a gospel that is greater than 100% with some small addition. This could include a gospel with added focus on guaranteed wealth and health in the here and now, or on specific additional rules and regulations that must be kept rather than trusting in the finished work of Christ on the cross, or on particular modern-day prophets who are imbued with a status of infallibility. All these might appear seemingly small, but they make a huge difference.

Yet the truth is that it is not just people 'out there' who proclaim a gospel that has had bits either removed or added. We can very easily do it ourselves – sometimes without even realizing it. Less than 100% and greater than 100% are equally dangerous.

I remember a conversation I once had with a woman at the end of a church service. She was a visitor from Latin America. When I asked her to tell me the issue she wanted to talk about, she replied, 'I am very sexy.' They weren't the first words I was expecting to hear! However, in her broken English, it transpired that she had been reading a Christian website which gave reports of individuals who had experienced visions of heaven and hell. One of the people who had had a vision reported how in hell there were lots of ladies wearing make-up and looking 'very sexy', and as a result of this, the internet site was telling women that they were forbidden to wear any jewellery or make-up. Of course, there was a right challenge to us all in that. Our beauty should come not from outward adornment, but from our inner self (1 Peter 3:3–4). But this legalistic requirement went way beyond the teaching of Scripture, and the unnecessary command that this woman throw out all her mascara and lipstick came about because she was not holding Scripture as her supreme authority. The internet site was proving a higher authority than the Bible.

I don't know what degree of authenticity there was in the visions of heaven and hell that she told me about. I certainly believe that God can and does from time to time give people visions or prophecies or words of knowledge. However, the problem comes if these revelations take on a greater authority than the supreme revelation of Scripture. The only place we can be 100% certain that we are hearing the very words of God is in the Bible.[1] Of course, all of Scripture needs to be rightly understood, and the Old Testament needs to be rightly interpreted through a Christological framework, but all other authorities, whether the wisdom of individuals or specific spiritual gifts, need to be tested against the written Word (see 1 Thessalonians 5:19–21). The 100% gospel will only flow when Scripture is held as the 100% supreme authority.

1. CHRISTIANITY IS 100% CHRIST

(Romans 1)

> Paul, a servant of Christ Jesus, called to be an apostle and
> set apart for the gospel of God – the gospel he promised
> beforehand through his prophets in the Holy Scriptures
> regarding his Son, who as to his human nature was a
> descendant of David, and who through the Spirit of
> holiness was declared with power to be the Son of God,
> by his resurrection from the dead: Jesus Christ our Lord.
> Through him and for his name's sake, we received grace
> and apostleship to call people from among all the Gentiles
> to the obedience that comes from faith. And you also are
> among those who are called to belong to Jesus Christ.
> (Romans 1:1–6 NIV 1984)

It was day four of my first job. I was working as a management consultant. I didn't have much idea what a management
consultant does, and here I was with a group of fifteen others,
at the beginning of a six-week intensive training programme
to discover the answer.

Everyone was out to impress both those higher up in the
firm and also each other. The boys were in their new pinstripe
suits. The girls were in their high heels. It felt like a cross
between a G8 summit and Freshers' Week. I had been given

a piece of flip-chart paper and a pen, and told to be ready in five minutes to present to the group on my answer to a question. The topic of the question surprised me. It seemed to have nothing to do with my new job at all: 'Who have been the three biggest influences in your life?'

I don't know what would have crossed your mind in this situation, but my first thoughts were these: 'I can't possibly mention Jesus', 'I'll be laughed out of town', 'I'll be eaten for breakfast', 'My new pinstripe suit will be toast'. In those five minutes, I prayed and cogitated and agonized about what to put on that giant rectangle of innocence that was waiting to be marked with my deliberations. Eventually, knowing I had to put something that declared my identity as a Christian, I put pen to paper, and wrote:

1. Mum
2. Dad
3. God

As I spoke to the group, I explained about the key influence my parents had had on me, and that God also had a huge influence on me because I was a Christian, and my faith was central to my identity. The deed had been done. Much to my relief, marmalade was not spread on my new suit.

A few weeks later, I was at a party and recounting this event to someone who was also a Christian. Immediately, she asked the killer question: 'Did you write "God" or "Jesus" on the flip chart?' Her question summarized why I had been feeling ambivalent about how I had tackled the situation. I was happy that I had, as it were, planted a marker in the sand to all my new colleagues about how I was a Christian. Yet I also had a nagging feeling that I had taken a fairly soft option. Not only had my parents come before my Lord in the list, but more tellingly, I had fallen short of mentioning Jesus' name. I had planted the marker, but it hadn't penetrated very deep into the sand, and was wobbling precariously in the breeze.

Christianity is 100% Christ. John Calvin declared, 'The whole gospel is contained in Christ . . . to move even a step from Christ means to withdraw oneself from the gospel.'[1] Calvin wrote this at the start of his commentary on the book of Romans. And he did so because Romans begins with the focus squarely on Jesus Christ. In the first sentence of the letter, Paul describes himself as 'a servant of Christ Jesus', and then continues to describe the gospel as something that is centred on the work and person of Jesus. Indeed, by the time we have read the introductory verses and got to Romans 1:9, where Paul summarizes his mission as 'preaching the gospel of [God's] Son', Jesus has already been mentioned eleven times.

Paul says he is 'called to be an apostle and set apart for the gospel of God' (Romans 1:1). None of us are now apostles in exactly the same sense that Paul was, but all followers of Christ are set apart for the gospel – whether we are called to be a management consultant, a medical student, a machine operator or whatever else we find ourselves involved in during life. Our faith is to be 100% focused and centred on Jesus Christ so that we don't move even a step from Christ, and so find ourselves withdrawing from the gospel.

Christ is the centre of the gospel

The reason for this bold challenge to be Christ-focused is that without him, this good news from God, who created the world and everything in it, has no meaning. Paul states that he was 'set apart for the gospel of God . . . regarding his Son' (Romans 1:1–3). God's good news is all about Jesus.[2]

It is of course vital that we give some content to this Jesus who is the centre of the gospel. Many varied and eclectic Jesuses have been paraded over the centuries since he walked this earth, some more faithful to the original than others. Despite challenges from some scholars, the most obvious place to go in search of the original Jesus is in the pages of the New Testament. Erasmus, the sixteenth-century theologian, wrote that the Bible 'will give Christ to you . . . in an intimacy so close that he would be less visible to you if he stood before your eyes'.[3]

1. Going down: At Jesus' birth, the Son of God took on human nature

Jesus did not come into being 2,000 ago at Bethlehem. He has always been, and always will be, the second person of the Trinity. Jesus' coming was not the result of a sudden decision, but had always been the one and only plan. We discover this in the Old Testament, which is not fundamentally a law book, but a promise book. It 'promised beforehand' what Jesus eventually came to do (Romans 1:2). The Old Testament shows us how God set things up between him and us, how it went wrong due to human rebellion, and most significantly how the promised coming of the Messiah would put things right between us and God. As John wrote in his Gospel, 'In the beginning was the Word, and the Word was with God, and the Word was God . . . In him was life, and that life was the light of [all people]. The light shines in the darkness, but the darkness has not understood it . . . The Word became flesh and made his dwelling among us' (John 1:1, 4–5, 14 NIV 1984). God did not choose a man to make his son, but he chose to make his one and only Son a man. God the Son has always been divine. Two thousand years ago, he took on human nature and became fully human as well as fully divine. He was both 'a descendant of David' and 'the Son of God' (Romans 1:3–4).

Despite all the genetic advances we read about in the press, no-one will ever decide to be born. But Jesus did. Remaining fully God, he became fully human. This is actually the most staggering claim of Christianity. So many people today say they struggle to believe in the miracles of Jesus, or that one man's death could really deal with our sin, or that Jesus really rose from the dead. But all those difficulties stem from not grasping the most remarkable claim of all: Jesus Christ was fully human *and* fully God.

My wife and I have three children, but there's a gap of six and a half years between our second and third child. When Susannah was twelve weeks pregnant with Hope, we told the older two that they were going to have another brother or sister. They couldn't believe it. Straight away, Boaz (aged six) said, with a nervous grin on his face, 'No you're not. You're joking!' We told him we were definitely speaking the truth, but he just couldn't believe it. We showed him how Susannah's tummy was slightly bigger, but he thought it was just because she had been eating too much.

Boaz couldn't believe it – until he saw the scan of his mum's tummy. With that image, the invisible suddenly became visible. In a sense, Jesus is like that scan. He makes the invisible God visible.

So take me. When I was seventeen, a friend badgered me to investigate Jesus. I thought Jesus was bad news – that he was boring, that he ruined your life. But I reluctantly followed my friend's advice. I was amazed at what I discovered as I read the Bible, heard talks about Jesus, and discussed the gospel with other people. Above all, I suddenly came face to face with the invisible God. As I read of Jesus calming the storm, I could see God's power. As I eavesdropped on Jesus' conversation with a woman who had had five husbands, I could see God's compassion. As I pictured in my mind Jesus' turning over the tables in the temple, I could see God's righteous anger. As I analysed Jesus' death on the cross in my place, I could see God's love. The invisible God became visible.

Ron Currie recently wrote a fictional book, *God Is Dead*, which is also about the invisible God becoming visible.[4] The inside front cover describes what the book is about:

> When God descends to earth as a Sudanese woman, and subsequently dies in the Darfur desert, the result is a world both fundamentally altered and yet eerily familiar. God – or Sora, as she's called – has come to earth to experience its conflicts first hand, but adopting a human form also means assuming human frailty and mortality . . . *God is Dead* is truly – and terrifyingly – original; blasphemous and heretical, it's an exceptional debut and a remarkable read.

It is true that you could call the book blasphemous and heretical, as it certainly contains some rather extraordinary ideas, but *God Is Dead* is in no way, as it claims, truly and terrifyingly original. Rather, it is a poor copy of what really happened. God did come down to earth. He did come into poverty and suffering and struggle. He did die.

This book isn't original at all. It's a copy. But it is a copy of only half the story.

2. Going up: At Jesus' resurrection, the Son of God took on power

Not only was there God the Son's going down all the way to death, but there was also God the Son's going up. Just like a yoyo, God the Son went down to come up.

Jesus was always the Son of God, and yet, through the work of the 'Spirit of holiness', the resurrection gave Jesus a new status. He 'was appointed to be the Son of God with power'

(Romans 1:4, NIV 1984 footnote translation).[5] Lesslie Newbigin wrote, 'The resurrection was not the reversal of a defeat but the manifestation of a victory.'[6] The resurrection, the culmination and validation of Christ's saving work on the cross, meant that the Son of God was given all power, not least as Judge and Saviour.

So when Paul was not writing a letter, but preaching to the people of Athens, he declared, '[God] has set a day when he will judge the world with justice by the man he has appointed. He has given proof of this to everyone by raising him from the dead' (Acts 17:31). Jesus' resurrection gives Jesus the power and authority to be Judge of us all. The Son of God is alive, and we will all meet him as he brings about total justice.

Yet the resurrection also allows Jesus to be Saviour. He can save us from judgment because, not only did he take the judgment that we deserve when he died on the cross in our place, but he also rose again, proving that his death was successful in fully dealing with our sin. As Paul wrote to the Corinthians, 'If Christ has not been raised, your faith is futile; you are still in your sins' (1 Corinthians 15:17). C. S. Lewis writes vividly:

In the Christian story, God descends to re-ascend. He comes down, down from the heights of absolute being into time and space, down into humanity, down to the very roots and seed bed of the humanity which He Himself created. But He goes down to come up again and bring ruined sinners up with Him . . . One has the picture of a strong man, stooping lower and lower to get himself underneath some great complicated burden. He must stoop in order to lift, he must almost disappear under the load before he incredibly straightens his back and marches off with the whole mass swaying on his shoulders.[7]

It is the original Jesus, the one who went down to death and up through resurrection, who can be our Saviour, as we place our faith in him.

Christ is the call of the gospel

It is because Jesus is the centre of the gospel that he is also the call of the gospel. The fundamental call on our lives is not to be religious or be good or be moral, but to 'belong to Jesus Christ' (Romans 1:6).

Daniel Radcliffe is most famous for playing Harry Potter, but he has also done a number of roles in theatre rather than film. One of these was the lead in Peter Shaffer's play, *Equus*. The plot concerns a boy who has a highly religious mother, and as a result he has a picture of Jesus on his bedroom wall. However, his father is an atheist who insists that this painting be taken down; it is then replaced by a picture of a horse. The devotion that the boy had given to the image of Jesus is now centred on the image of the horse, and this leads to the father sending his son to a psychiatrist. At one point the psychiatrist declares, 'Without worship, you shrink.' His message is that it doesn't matter what we worship, as long as we worship something.

Christianity says something very different. It says it matters intensely what we worship. Indeed, Paul says it is idolatry when we worship any other thing or purpose or person than Jesus Christ (Romans 1:25). This matters because it is an offence to Jesus, but it also matters because nothing else can fully deliver. *The Times* columnist, Matthew Parris, who says he is not a Christian, understands the problem of idolatry. He wrote about President Obama at the height of his popularity:

He, we sense, understands. He cares. He is like us, understands
us, surely agrees with us, though he has not yet said so. He
would be our friend if ever we were to meet him. In some
strange way, he knows us already . . . He is the pop star whose
poster adorns the adolescent's bedroom wall; the Blessed Mary
who understands her supplicant's every woe . . . the Queen
Mother who, had she ever come to tea, would have got on with
us like a house on fire. It is desperately important that we never
meet these people, for reality would be cruel . . . Believe me, the
disillusion when Elton John looks bored to meet you and turns
away can be bitter.[8]

Whether it is the poster of the pop star or the picture of the
horse, whether Barack Obama or Elton John, no idol can
ever provide us with all we desire. Yet the Christian claim
is that the reality of meeting Jesus is far from cruel. He can
and does deliver. It is not a lack of worship that makes
us shrink. Rather, it is a lack of the worship of Jesus that
shrinks us.

Money. Family. Success. Happiness. All these are good
things, but it is foolish to make any of these the ultimate thing
– the Lord – in our life. They can't provide complete fulfilment, and they certainly can't provide forgiveness. Above all,
we are to belong to Jesus and worship him.

'Jesus Christ our Lord' (Romans 1:4) is perhaps the best
short summary of the gospel that there is. Jesus was his
human name, but it was given for a specific reason – because
it means 'the Lord saves' (Matthew 1:21). Christ means 'the
Anointed One', referring to the Messiah that the people of
Israel were waiting for who would deliver his people. 'Lord',
used of Jesus, speaks of the one who is God and who has
authority to rule over this world and each one of us. These
summary titles of Jesus remind us that it is not just who Jesus

is that makes the gospel good news, but also what he has *done*. Jesus is good news because the perfect Son of God came down to earth, died a death in our place, and rose to life in total power as Lord of all. Without Christ, there is no good news. He is the centre and the call.

Dog lovers in Argentina were recently delighted to buy fashionable toy poodles for a few hundred dollars – only to later discover that their beloved poodles were actually ferrets who had had their fur blow-dried, and then been fed steroids to make them grow bigger.[9] What these people thought was good news turned out to be very bad news.

With Christianity, it is the opposite. So often, Christianity is viewed as bad news. Certainly, in the media, Christianity gets a bad press. It's seen as restrictive, boring, irrelevant, untrue, bigoted. Even among Christians, we can start thinking that our faith is bad news. Yet the reality is that there is no greater news than the Christian gospel. What is seen to be bad news is actually the best news ever – what we thought was a ferret is actually a poodle.

This is 100% due to Jesus Christ. John Stott brilliantly summarizes:

> The person and work of Christ are the rock upon which the Christian religion is built. If he is not who he said he was, and if he did not do what he said he had come to do, the foundation is undermined and the whole superstructure will collapse. Take Christ from Christianity, and you disembowel it; there is practically nothing left. Christ is the centre of Christianity; all else is circumference.[10]

When I next have to write the three biggest influences in my life on a flip chart, in whatever circumstances and with whatever repercussions, I hope that I will not be ashamed of the gospel, and that at number one on the list I will write the name of the one who is the centre and the call of the gospel. We are 'called to belong to Jesus Christ' (Romans 1:6).

100% activation

I met Jesus when I was eighteen. Up until that point, I just hadn't thought much about him, which is strange given that I'd grown up going to 'Christian' schools and had sung countless anthems to him in chapel choirs.

Before that point, life had been a mix of highs and lows, of good times and bad. I came from a very loving family, but my parents' marriage came to an end when I was nine, leaving me hurt and confused. I'd had the best education money could buy. I played as much sport as I could, had lots of fun and friends, but for all of those positives, I just wasn't satisfied. This sense of turmoil 'within' would often manifest itself 'without', and I could be angry and aggressive. As a form of escapism, and also because I enjoyed it, I smoked a lot of weed from the age of fifteen onwards. I began to experiment with harder drugs, but fortunately couldn't afford many of them!

It was during this time of adolescent angst, from seventeen onwards, that I began asking lots of questions: Why are we here? Is there a God? What happens when we die? Do I have to be an accountant?! I just didn't have the answers (well, I knew I didn't want to be an accountant).

I soon discovered that a friend of mine was a Christian, so I began firing all my questions at him and we'd discuss things between lessons. The more I enquired, the more I got interested. I began reading about all the different religions, increasingly convinced there must be answers. And if I'm honest, I hoped God was real, as I didn't much like the person I'd become and knew I wanted to change. I knew I needed forgiveness and healing and that only God could do it.

I began going along to the school Christian Union with my friend Dave. He also took me to his church in London a couple of times. As I began to hear the Bible taught, there'd be times when it felt like the preacher was speaking directly to me as he explained the human condition, and God's response to it in the person of Jesus. Hope began to stir.

After a while, Dave invited me to go on a 'Christian camp' in the Easter holidays. I curiously said yes. It was there that my life changed for ever. Not only did I hear the gospel clearly explained, but I also saw the life that Jesus offers embodied in the people around me. You see, I understood Christianity by then, but I still didn't know Jesus Christ. I saw his life and joy in the teenagers around me, but knew I didn't have it in myself. On the third evening, we heard a talk on the evidence for the resurrection. I'd never heard it explained so reasonably. As the leader spoke, it was as if my eyes were opened as I realized that Jesus must still be alive, and if he was alive, then I could know him.

I excitedly went back to my room, knowing that I was about to reach out to a God I'd never met, but who I now believed was there. So at 12.30 am, after reading my Bible for a bit in bed, I prayed a prayer that changed my life. At first it felt like I was talking to the ceiling, but I did it anyway, praying from the heart, offering God everything. No sooner had I prayed than I was filled with an overwhelming sense of love and joy and peace. It literally felt as if a charge of electricity flowed through my body (in a nice way!), causing me to arch up on my heels and shoulder blades. I'd never felt such love and peace, and, man, did I feel happy! I knew it was what I'd been searching for. The next day, the familiar scowl I'd often worn had been replaced by a grin that has barely left me since. A guy at the camp couldn't believe what had happened to me, saying I'd lit up like a light bulb! I guess that's how I felt.

I knew right then that I wanted to spend the rest of my life telling people about Jesus. I was convinced he's what everybody's looking for. (I'm now a vicar, so you could say I'm 'living the dream'. Don't let that put you off!) Since then, it's been an adventure of faith as I've sought to follow Christ. It hasn't all been easy, and there have been challenges on the way, but I'd never go back to a life without Christ. In him, we've got it all.

(Pat Allerton, vicar)

100% adoration

Jesus, thank you that the Christian gospel is good news.
Thank you that this is all because of you.
Help me see God's power and compassion and truth and justice
        and love in you.
Thank you that supremely you don't call me to be good, or
        moral, or religious,
but that you call me to belong to you.
Thank you for who you are and all that you have done for me.
Help me not to be ashamed of you and your gospel.
Amen.

1. Christianity is 100% Christ

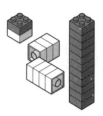

Christ is the **centre** of the Gospel *(1:1–4)*
- *Going down:* at Jesus' birth, he took on human nature
- *Going up:* at Jesus' birth, he took on power

Christ is the **call** of the Gospel *(1:5–6)*

 'Jesus Christ our Lord' *(Romans 1:4)*
- the centre and the call
- the reason Christianity is good news

100% application

1. Do you find it difficult to believe that Jesus is fully human and fully God?
2. In your experience, how does Jesus make the invisible God visible?
3. What does it mean to you to 'belong to Jesus Christ' (Romans 1:6)?
4. What would you write on a flip chart in response to the question: 'Who have been the three biggest influences in your life?'

Read Romans 1.

2. CHRISTIANITY IS 100% CRITICAL

(Romans 1 – 3)

> Therefore no one will be declared righteous in God's sight
> by the works of the law; rather, through the law we become
> conscious of our sin. But now apart from the law the
> righteousness of God has been made known, to which the
> Law and the Prophets testify. This righteousness is given
> through faith in Jesus Christ to all who believe. There is no
> difference between Jew and Gentile, for all have sinned and
> fall short of the glory of God, and all are justified freely by
> his grace through the redemption that came by Christ Jesus.
> (Romans 3:20–24)

'It *was* all going so well . . .'

Astute individual that I am, the emphasis on the word
'was' alerted me to the fact that this was going to be a challenging question. I had just given a talk to a group of people
who were beginning to investigate the Christian faith at the
start of an Alpha course. We'd moved on to the Question-
and-Answer time afterwards over coffee, and a woman in her
thirties had just put up her hand: 'It *was* all going so well. I
loved everything you said, but then you had to go and spoil
it by talking about eternal life. I love all the stuff about how
Christianity has a positive effect in this life, but why do we

need to worry about these unfashionable things like heaven
and hell and judgment?'

This woman did have a valid point. The Christian gospel is
not merely about obtaining a ticket to heaven when I die.
That's an incomplete message. It leads to Christians separating themselves off from the world, 'waiting' until they get
to the wonder of heaven. Christianity should have an impact
in the here and now. Francis Schaeffer commented that
Christianity 'is a life and death struggle over the minds and
souls of men for eternity, but it is equally a life and death
struggle over life on this earth'.[1]

Christianity has a personal impact, enabling us to know 'life
in all its fullness' (John 10:10 GNT) now, through a relationship
with God.

Christianity also has a public impact, causing us to 'love our
neighbour as ourselves' (Matthew 22:39), to look out for the
poor, to want God's kingdom to come 'on earth as it is in
heaven' (Matthew 6:10). Nonetheless, a Christianity that
focuses merely on the present, whether on our personal
spiritual experience, or our practical impact, but which leaves
out the question of eternity, is totally deficient. One hundred
per cent Christianity must include the life-and-death struggle
over the minds, souls and bodies of us all for eternity.

My response to this woman wasn't perfect. I generally find
in these situations that I think of what I should have said a few
hours too late. But the main thing I did say rather surprised her.
I told her that I could not believe in a God if he were not a God
of wrath and judgment. God values each one of us so much
that he thinks it matters how I treat you and how you treat me
and how we all treat one another. The existence of God's wrath
is a good thing. The reality is that if all the evil that happens in
this world took place, and it were to go unnoticed by God, then
he could definitely not be a God of love.

In August 2011, there were riots all across London. There was one on the road next to where I was living. The area was cordoned off as a crime scene due to the rioting and looting of youths. Obviously, local residents were upset by the looters, but what was interesting was that they were also upset with the police and politicians. They felt there wasn't a large enough police presence, and were angry that all the key politicians were away on their summer holidays. It seemed as if those in authority did not care enough about them, because they weren't present and displaying their 'wrath' towards the looters. People felt unloved. It would be exactly the same if God did not care about wrongdoing. We only know he is a God of love because he can be bothered to act in judgment against evil.

Of course, I am very aware that the very mention of God's wrath and judgment raises people's eyebrows, and their hackles too, just as it did with the woman at the talk. She would have been very disappointed with the apostle Paul. It only takes him seventeen verses of his letter to the Romans before he starts talking about 'the wrath of God'. In fact, God's judgment is the major theme of the first three chapters of his letter.

The problem of God's wrath

We need to be clear what the Bible means. God's wrath is not the same as sinful human anger, which is often an irrational, uncontrollable emotion. God's wrath is not 'flying off the handle'. It is not a fury boiling over, complete with feelings of revenge towards someone. Rather God's wrath is best defined as his holy hostility to evil.

Paul declares that 'the wrath of God is being revealed from heaven against all the godlessness and wickedness of [those] who suppress the truth by their wickedness' (Romans 1:18 NIV 1984). This has to be a good thing. Our world is full of injustice. Good people suffer and evil people prosper. Joseph Stalin, for example, was responsible for the murder of millions and yet he died in old age in his bed, while many others have suffered or died in the prime of life as a result of the actions of others. In a world of unchecked injustice, God's wrath satisfies our need for justice.

However, the existence of God's wrath also has personal implications for us all. Everyone, without exception, faces God's wrath. Paul writes that 'they exchanged the truth of God for a lie, and worshipped and served created things rather than the Creator' (Romans 1:25), and the reality is that this is a description of every single one of us.

Recently, I was driving our eldest two children to school on the other side of Clapham Common in London, when we passed Ladbrokes, the betting shop. 'Daddy, what's Ladbrokes?', pipes up Daisy, aged seven.

'It's a betting shop,' I explain. 'Where people gamble.'

'Like Grandpa does on the horses,' she says.

'Yes . . . but he only does it occasionally,' I reply, trying to prevent my daughter from growing up viewing her grandfather as a non-stop gambling machine (which he is not!).

'Is it wrong?' she asked.

And so I started talking about how some things were addictive, and how once you did them, you kept on wanting to do them more and more. 'Gambling is a bit like that,' I said. 'So too is smoking cigarettes. People find they get addicted to that.'

There was a pause. Then Daisy verbalized her thinking: 'I'm addicted to my guinea pigs.'

So I tried to explain that generally one used the word 'addicted' when it was a bad thing that someone kept on wanting more. But, rather getting into the swing of the conversation, I continued by saying that sometimes even good things – like guinea pigs – can become such a large focus for us that we make them more of a priority than God, and that God should be our number one addiction.

Daisy rather liked this idea, and so she started compiling her top ten addictions.

'Number one,' she said, 'is God. Number two . . . is Pumpkin' (her guinea pig). 'Number three . . . is Mummy. Number four . . . is Patch' – Boaz's guinea pig.

By the time I came in at number nine in her top ten addictions, I was getting highly offended.

But while this had been going on, Boaz had just been quiet, listening to the conversation, taking it all in. He then decided to enter into the discussion.

'I'm addicted to me,' said Boaz.

In one sentence, my son had managed to define the essence of sin: being addicted to ourselves. Putting God out of the equation. We turn our backs on God, the Creator, and become far more interested in the things he has created and which we turn to in search of fulfilment: money, success, football, holidays.

It is because these created things become our gods as we put ourselves at the centre of the universe that we all deserve God's wrath. According to Paul, this is true even for those who have never heard about Jesus. Paul writes, 'For since the creation of the world God's invisible qualities – his eternal power and divine nature – have been clearly seen, being understood from what has been made, so that people are without excuse' (Romans 1:20). Just to make sure we have understood his point, after listing all sorts of different types of people, including the good, the moral and the religious, Paul concludes his initial thesis as follows: 'What shall we conclude then? Are we any better? Not at all! We have already made the charge that Jews and Gentiles alike are all under sin. As it is written: "There is no-one righteous, not even one"' (Romans 3:9–10 NIV 1984). The verdict is that everyone, without exception, faces God's wrath.

Alexander Solzhenitsyn, the Russian novelist and historian who won the Nobel Prize for Literature in 1970, wrote these poignant and famous words: 'If only there were evil people somewhere insidiously committing evil deeds, and it were necessary only to separate them from the rest of us and destroy them. But the line dividing good and evil cuts through the heart of every human being.'² There is undoubtedly good in every human, for we are all created in the image of God. But there is just as undoubtedly evil in everyone as well, and we are rightly held accountable for this evil. We all face judgment. Paul anticipates the scene on Judgment Day, and there is a fearful hush with every mouth silenced: 'Now we know that whatever the law says, it says to those who are under the law, so that every mouth may be silenced and the whole world held accountable to God. Therefore no-one will be declared righteous in his sight by observing the law' (Romans 3:19–20 NIV 1984).

Julian Barnes, the brilliant author, social commentator and Booker Prize winner, has written a book about his thoughts on death. It is, to quote him, 'a meditation on mortality'. The opening line is memorable: 'I don't believe in God, but I miss Him.'³ Barnes' book is sentimental, and sweet, but I fear it is also wrong. Its title is: *Nothing to Be Frightened Of*, but the truth is that there is something about which we should have a right fear. We are all sinful, and, as a result, under God's wrath. We are without excuse, and we face God's judgment. It is a huge problem. We must all face up to it.

I remember once speaking at a church event where there was someone who had come to help serve the coffee. This man had recently joined the church community and, wonderfully, had become a Christian. But he had a problem – he was an alcoholic. When I met him, he'd had a bad time the previous night. Something had gone wrong, and as a result he had bought himself a bottle of vodka and drunk the whole contents. When I chatted to him, he was still drunk, and he had been told he couldn't help serve at the event that day. He was in a bad way emotionally. There was little positive about the situation. But there was one positive: he had faced up to his problem. As we talked, he said to me, straight out, that he was an alcoholic. He wasn't hiding it or repressing it.

So often, when it comes to the problem we all have, as objects of God's wrath, we try to pretend it doesn't exist. The first step towards an alcoholic's recovery is to admit the existence of the problem. Similarly, it is only when we each admit the existence of our problem that we will turn to find the solution.

The solution to God's wrath

Christianity is 100% critical because we all share this desperate problem, and the Christian gospel is the only solution. In his letter to the Christians in Rome, Paul is challenging those who act as though they are morally or socially superior to others. Some of these first-century Christians thought that their good works, religious observance or Jewish pedigree made them better in God's eyes. It is very easy to slip into that mentality, but the reality is that we can't do anything to solve the problem of God's wrath ourselves. The ball is in God's court. It is up to God whether he wants to forgive us, and the answer that is at the heart of the gospel is that, amazingly, he *does* want to forgive us, and he has provided a solution which enables his perfect standard of justice to be maintained alongside his perfect standard of love.

God's solution is the death of his own Son on the cross. It is Jesus' death which enables us to be seen as righteous in God's eyes, no longer needing to face the just consequences of God's holy hostility towards all that is evil. On the cross, God's holy hostility to evil was directed at Jesus instead of us. Paul writes that 'God presented [Jesus] as the one who would turn aside [God's] wrath, taking away sin' (Romans 3:25 NIV 1984, footnote translation). As a result of Jesus' act, the righteousness of God can come to us all 'through faith in Jesus Christ to all who believe' (Romans 3:22). There is now no need to fear facing judgment. Through faith in Jesus, all fear at having to face God's wrath can evaporate, because Jesus has faced God's holy hostility on our behalf.

I have few claims to fame, but one of them is that I have been the understudy of a famous pop star. If you were to get to know me, you would be very surprised by this, because I can't sing – I can only growl. The best evidence for this is that when I was ten, I was thrown out of the junior choir at school. To this day I can remember the music teacher's words: 'Jago, I'm afraid we are going to have to ask you to leave the choir. Your voice doesn't quite fit in with everybody else's.' Yet, despite my vocal limitations, I was still the understudy for someone who has sold over 18 million albums, won two Brit Awards and was voted Hottest Male in the 2010 Virgin Media Music Awards.

Actually, this was also when I was ten – a few months after being thrown out of the choir. James Blunt, he of 'You're Beautiful' fame, was the lead part, Jim Hawkins, in our school play, *Treasure Island*. A couple of days before the play he was swinging on a loo door, as you do, and fell off and got concussed. Much to his annoyance, he was not well enough on the first night, and so I had to take his part, book in hand.

I was James Blunt's substitute. In the school play, I took his part. In the gospel, Jesus Christ took our part. He is our substitute – not on the wooden boards of a school play, but on the wooden boards of a Roman cross. He died in our place. His death is the solution to our problem of us deserving God's wrath. It is a solution that took place because of God's love for you and for me.

In a typical Anglican liturgy, the prayer of confession speaks to God of 'the grievous sins and wickedness which we have so often committed by thought, word and deed against your divine majesty, provoking most justly your anger and indignation against us'. We each have sinned in our thoughts, words and deeds. The wonder is that the good news of Jesus' death on our behalf is the solution to the problem of our sin. Yet, not only does it provide a solution, it also enables a transformation to occur in these three same areas: our thoughts, words and deeds.

1. Our thoughts

So often, the world's view of Christianity is that Christians are rather critical and self-righteous, looking down on others. Yet it is a great travesty for Christians to be critical of others, to think that we are in any way better than or superior to others. The reality is that who we are or what we do does not make the slightest bit of difference in trying to get right with God. We all naturally deserve God's wrath. It is only through faith in Christ that we get to be in a right relationship with God. It's not about what we do, but about what Jesus has done for us. Paul declares, 'Where, then, is boasting? It is excluded. On what principle? On that of observing the law? No, but on that of faith. For we maintain that a [person] is justified by faith apart from observing the law' (Romans 3:27–28 NIV 1984). If the gospel doesn't keep us humble in our thinking, nothing will.

2. Our words

One of the biggest dangers for Christianity in the twenty-first century is that we don't mention the problem we all face. We can often find ourselves telling people that Jesus is the solution to all their problems, but we never actually make it clear what those problems are. Each one of us was created for a relationship with God. There is a hole inside us all which can only be filled by God. Yet if we think that hole is merely a need for meaning and purpose in life, or a need to feel loved, or a need for healing, or a need to have a sense of peace, then there is a significant problem. Yes, Jesus does provide purpose and love and peace. Yes, Jesus does sometimes heal, sometimes miraculously. Yet if those are the only problems that Christianity solves, then not everyone needs it.

Take Julian Barnes. I have never met him, but I greatly admire him and his writing. It is amazing that he is willing to write so frankly about the whole subject of death, and with such vulnerability. As far as I am aware, Julian Barnes is neither lacking purpose in life, nor ill, nor unloved. So if the Christianity that he is presented with only tries to solve those things, then he has no urgent need of it. He writes that he misses God, but I think that his yearning to be in a right relationship with God would be far greater if he were clearer about the fundamental problem that the gospel solves.

Christianity only becomes critical to everyone when we are clear that the fundamental problem that it solves is the problem of us all facing God's wrath because we have all sinned and fallen short of the glory of God. We need to use words to tell people, in love, the ultimate problem that we all face, and the good news that the gospel offers.

3. Our deeds

Alexander Solzhenitsyn wrote those words – 'the line dividing good and evil cuts through the heart of every human being' – in his famous book, *The Gulag Archipelago*. It is a three-volume tome examining the Soviet prison camp system that he himself had experienced. He was imprisoned under Stalin for writing poetry. It was in that prison camp that Solzhenitsyn witnessed two Christian pastors being beaten up by the prison guards, and killed. As he saw the way these men met their deaths, he was mesmerized by how gracefully they suffered and died. As a result of that incident, he decided to become a Christian.

Those two pastors were consistent in living out their faith. The gospel changed their deeds and actions. They weren't taking off the red Lego block of their Christian faith when the going was tough and there was a cost to their faith. They knew it was 100% critical. With the apostle Paul they were saying in their actions: 'I'm not ashamed of the gospel.'

100% activation

Growing up going to church in Australia, two main things kept baffling me: why did Christians love Jesus so much, and why on earth was Jesus' death the focus of Christianity? A guy at church had the word 'Jesus' on his guitar strap, and 'JESUS' was written in big letters at the front of my grandma's church. Quite frankly, I was rather embarrassed by this. You see, my faith only consisted of a relationship with God, not Jesus, and was only kept for emergencies. It was like God was in my 'only use when needed' box – exam time, school leadership election time, boyfriend time – just the important things like that. Friends knew that I was a little different from them, doing everything

in moderation, and saying 'Gosh' instead of 'God', but that
was about it.

After uni, I moved to London, and I was determined to
distance myself from anything to do with Christianity. I didn't
really understand who Jesus was, I didn't understand why his
death was significant, and I thought the Bible was a waste of
time. I started working at a law firm and life felt like one big
party, but it wasn't long until God started closing in. Annoyingly,
not long after I started there, I met a Christian girl who was very
kind to me and, as if that wasn't enough, I discovered that the
boy who lived next door to me (who is now married to my
sister!) was a Christian too. In fact, he also went to the same
church as my friend from work. The Christians were definitely
closing in!

Annoyed as I was, I somehow agreed to go to a lunchtime talk
about Christianity with this girl from work. This was the first
time I'd heard the Bible being explained verse by verse and I was
really intrigued and so kept going back, week on week. Soon
I was encouraged to go along to a course called 'Christianity
Explored'. In my head I was thinking I'd explored it enough
and was a sorted Christian anyway, but they all seemed very
enthusiastic, so I reluctantly agreed to go.

Unfortunately I wasn't a model course attendee, and only went
for two weeks. I distinctly remember swanning in to one of those
two sessions, thinking that I'd missed it anyway, and found myself
around a table where everyone was talking about sin. People were
actually admitting they were sinful. I couldn't believe it, and I told
everyone else I didn't think I was a sinner. You see, my heart and
mind were totally oblivious to the fact that the essence of sin is a
rejection of God's rule over my life. The fact that I'd always put
God in my only-use-when-needed box was a sin.

A couple of months later, I found myself at a Bible study
weekend focusing on Jesus' death on the cross. Again, this meant

nothing to me until I suddenly realized that this whole sin thing was why Jesus died – to take the punishment for the whole world's sins. That weekend, in February 2000, I was so cross at what I'd heard, but I knew it was true and that I had to make a decision. I'd finally realized I needed to be saved like everybody else.

That evening, I ran outside into the dark by myself, and said to God, 'Fine then, have it your way; have my life.' To my surprise nothing spectacular happened, except that I had a sense that I'd done what I needed to do. A month or two later, I remember hearing a sermon where the preacher said, 'Perhaps you're someone for whom God has recently switched the lights on.' Those words came thundering at me and I knew God had taken me from a life of self-righteousness to the life I was made for – in a right relationship with God through Jesus. I was so excited. I wanted to tell everyone I met about Jesus' giant rescue plan. No longer was God just in my only-use-when-needed box; he was at the centre of my life.

Since then, life has had its up and downs, and in so many ways I don't live the way God would want me to, but I know that I'm certain of his help in this life, and I'm certain of spending eternity with him in heaven. Not because of anything I've done, but because of what Jesus has done for me.
(Kate Riley, full-time mum)

100% adoration

Heavenly Father, I've thought about the serious subject of
    your wrath
  – your holy hostility to all evil.
Yet I praise you that it is against this dark backdrop that the light
    and the radiance of the good news of Christ crucified
    shines all the more brightly.

May I increasingly realize that I need you more than
    anything else,
and that it is 100% critical to put my trust in you.
By the power of your Spirit,
    make me humble,
    keep me speaking about the problem and the solution,
    and keep me consistent in my deeds and actions as I live
        for you.
In Jesus' name I pray.
Amen.

2. Christianity is 100% critical

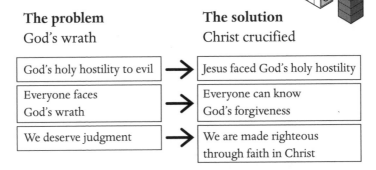

The problem
God's wrath

The solution
Christ crucified

God's holy hostility to evil	→	Jesus faced God's holy hostility
Everyone faces God's wrath	→	Everyone can know God's forgiveness
We deserve judgment	→	We are made righteous through faith in Christ

This changes our **thoughts**, **words** and **deeds**

100% application

1. 'I could not believe in a God if he were not a God of wrath and judgment.' Do you agree?
2. What evidence is there that 'the line dividing good and evil cuts through the heart of every human being'?

3. What problem is Jesus the solution to?
4. How will this chapter have an impact on how you speak about Jesus with your friends and families and work colleagues?

Read Romans 2 – 3.

3. CHRISTIANITY IS 100% CREDIBLE

(Romans 4 – 5)

> Blessed are those
>> whose transgressions are forgiven,
>> whose sins are covered.
> Blessed is the one whose sin the Lord will never count
>> against them.
> (Romans 4:7–8)

The Samaria Gorge in Crete is 10 miles (16 km) long and takes about five hours to negotiate. At places the gorge is incredibly narrow, just 4 metres across, but 300 metres high.

My first visit to the gorge was unusually hair-raising. I was with three friends, walking through the narrowest bit of the gorge, with me at the front, when suddenly a small rock clattered on the floor a couple of paces in front of me. I was a little perturbed, but assumed it was just a freak fall. However, a few minutes later, the same thing happened.

This was no time to panic. I took command, and told my three friends that we needed to put our rucksacks on top of our heads to protect ourselves. You can picture the scene. The four of us, nervously walking down the gorge, bags on our heads. And every ten minutes or so there would be yet another rock fall.

Now, I did geography at university, high-intellect subject that it is, so my friends started asking me why this rock fall was happening. I vaguely remembered hearing something about erosion taking place as a result of mountain goats, and we had seen quite a lot of goats on our walk. I therefore explained to my ignorant companions that it was due to the goats, grazing high above and dislodging the rocks.

And so we continued. Walking, bags still on heads, rocks still falling from time to time, until eventually, after five hours of walking, we reached the end of the gorge – exhausted physically and emotionally – but safe! It was a huge relief.

But later that evening I discovered that the cause of the falling rocks had not been hairy four-legged friends high up in the gorge, but my three not quite so hairy two-legged friends lobbing rocks over my head. For five hours!

Many people today would say that anyone who is religious is just like me in that gorge. In their opinion, a religious person looks around at the environment he or she lives in, and then comes up with strange explanations as deluded as my idea about mountain goats.

This may surprise you, but I would agree with that view! Plenty of religious and spiritual beliefs are as deluded as my mountain goat theory. They have to be. Muslims believe in one God. So do Christians, and yet Muslims disagree when Christians speak of the Trinity. Hindus believe in many gods. Many Buddhists believe in no God. Christian Scientists believe that God is just a principle. They can't all be right. Many ideas about God must be deluded in some way.

In Richard Dawkins' book, *The God Delusion*, a key plank of his argument in attacking religion and the existence of God is that all religions are by and large the same. He writes, 'For my purposes the differences matter less than the similarities.'[1] However, that is the crucial fallacy in his whole argument, because the reality is that there are huge differences between religions. This does matter a great deal.

Only Christianity dares to make God's love totally unconditional, saying that we don't have to earn God's love, for it comes to us with no strings attached – justification by faith. All the other religions of the world say that our relationship with the universal deity (if they believe in one) is at least partly dependent on our own efforts – justification by works. The question is: which of the two options, if either, is credible?

The rationale for justification by faith

I mentioned Stalin in the previous chapter, so let's refer him to him once more. Just suppose that he, the night before he died in old age asleep in his bed, after committing so many evil acts throughout his life, decided to put his trust in Jesus. As far as I am aware this did not happen, but if that was the case, then, according to the Christian faith, Stalin would now be in heaven. This sounds very unfair, unreasonable and far from credible. What about all the people who have done lots of good things in the world – but haven't put their faith in Jesus? It sounds like Christianity is as ludicrous as my disastrous mountain goat theory.

This hypothetical situation gets to the heart of the debate about justification. The simple Sunday school definition of being 'justified' is that God views me now 'just as if I'd' never sinned. Recent theologians have reminded us that justification does not just have a mere pietistic focus on the present relationship between an individual and God, but is integrated within the whole biblical narrative.[2] However, the way we are made right with God is still at the very heart of what justification is about. The crucial question is whether it makes more sense for us to be able to get into a right relationship with God through our own works, or through faith in Jesus' work.

1. Justification by faith shows that God is not fickle
(Romans 4:1–8)
There are lots of ways that humans are fickle. Whether it is fashion changing over the years, or footballers swapping their club allegiance for the right financial incentive, it is clear that we often change in our desires and longings. In many instances, it is not too serious for us to be fickle, but it would be serious if God were like that. God must be constant and be the same yesterday, today and for ever (Hebrews 13:8). He must be constantly perfect, rather than changing over time.

Yet God seems to be fickle. After all, in Jesus' time, all the religious leaders seemed to be saying that the Old Testament was all about justification by good works. Jesus' parable of the Pharisee and the tax collector perhaps best illustrates this (Luke 18:9–14). Two men go to the temple to pray, and the Pharisee tells God that he has not done bad things (robbery, evil, adultery) and that he has done good things (fasting, giving). The Pharisees thought they were justified by their works. However, the message of Jesus, and the message of the apostles as recorded in the rest of the New Testament, was that God saves people by faith, not works. While the Pharisee declared his good works to God, 'the tax collector stood at a distance. He would not even look up to heaven, but beat his breast and said, "God, have mercy on me, a sinner"' (Luke 18:13). Jesus' verdict was as follows: 'I tell you that this man, rather than the other, went home justified before God' (Luke 18:14). The tax collector went home justified because

CHRISTIANITY IS 100% CREDIBLE

he put his faith in God's mercy, rather than his own good works. Jesus taught justification by faith.

So how can God change? He seems to be fickle and inconsistent, changing the way to get right with him over time. Until 2,000 years ago, justification by works was all the rage, and then – a sudden switch with Jesus, the fashion altering faster than a move from a mini to a maxi dress. God fancied a change, and suddenly, justification by faith is the way to go.

Paul, a Jew himself, answers this challenge in a way that may surprise you. He declares that the Old Testament does not, and never has, suggested that people get right with God by their good works. Even in Old Testament times, people were justified by faith in God and not by their works. Paul gives two examples of this from the Old Testament to back up his claim.

First, Abraham. Paul writes, 'If, in fact, Abraham was justified by works, he had something to boast about – but not before God. What does the Scripture say? "Abraham believed God, and it was credited to him as righteousness"' (Romans 4:2–3). In other words, it was not by works that Abraham got right with God, but rather by believing in God and having faith in him.

Second, David. Paul declares that David 'speaks of the blessedness of [those] to whom God credits righteousness apart from works' (Romans 4:6 NIV 1984). In both instances, we see that these two Old Testament heroes were given a right relationship with God through faith, rather than any specific works.

God has never changed his mind over how we should get into a right relationship with him. He is not fickle. Since the very first human, the way to get right with God has always been the same. It is not, and it never has been, through what we do. It has always been through faith in what God has done.

2. Justification by faith shows that God does not have favourites (Romans 4:9–25)

We all hate it when someone who is supposed to be impartial shows favouritism. Our eldest two children – Daisy and Boaz – demonstrate this regularly. If I give one of them one more sweet or one more piggyback or one more cuddle, then the other is incensed: 'She's got more than me!' 'He's had three goes and I've only had two!' It has to be fair. Daisy and Boaz know that it is wrong to show favouritism.

Yet, by its very nature, justification by works has to involve God showing favouritism to some people over others. It might be favouritism to the people who pray more than others, or favouritism to the people who pray facing the right direction, or favouritism to the people who conduct the right sort of penance that most impresses God.

Particularly in the context of Paul's letter to the Romans, it looks like the Jews are God's favourites. In academic circles today, there are big debates about what the main thinking was among the Jewish people back in the first century. Were they looking to get right with God through moral performance (such as keeping the Ten Commandments), or through religious performance (such as getting circumcised), or through just being born into a certain ethnic group (the Jews)? Different theologians argue about which was most important, but to be honest it doesn't matter which is the main one because, whichever it is, underneath all three of these possibilities, the claim is that a person gets right with God through something that depends on him or her.

It is into this debate that Paul says that the reality is that God is the God of everybody – Jew and non-Jew (see, for example, Romans 3:29–31) – and everyone can be brought into a right relationship with God on exactly the same basis. That same basis is faith. There's no favouritism. So take

Abraham again. He got into a right relationship with God way before he got the knife out to perform the ritual of circumcision. It wasn't about performing some special religious act that enabled him to be right with God; it was simple faith in God (Romans 4:9–10).

Anyone can get right with God – circumcised or uncircumcised, genius or dunce, rich or poor. Anyone – through faith.

3. Justification by faith means that God is faithful (Romans 5:1–11)

Imagine we met one evening for a drink, and I said that I promised to give you a billion pounds, a luxury villa in the south of France and a top-of-the-range yacht. You would be very contented as you sipped on your favourite tipple. But then imagine I continued by saying that I promised to give you all those things . . . as long as you could fly to the moon and back by midnight. That would cause you to sit up with a start, wouldn't it? Because, when I say that, then my promises become a waste of space.

That is exactly the same situation if God operates on the principle that people are justified by their works. God holds out the most amazing gift to each one of us, better even than a house, a boat and a billion quid. His gift to us is peace with him in the present (Romans 5:1) and protection from his wrath in the future (Romans 5:9).

God's gift to us is mind-blowing. There is nothing greater. However, it is only mind-blowing if it is a genuine gift. If we had to work to get peace with God and protection from God's wrath, then we would never manage it. It would be impossible and totally out of our reach – like having to travel to the moon and back by midnight.

The only way we can know that we are guaranteed this amazing gift, and that God will be faithful to us and give us

what he has promised us, is if receiving the gift doesn't depend
on our performance. And sure enough, Paul writes, 'Therefore,
since we have been *justified through faith*, we have peace with
God' (Romans 5:1), and 'since we have now been *justified by
his blood*, how much more shall we be saved from God's wrath'
(Romans 5:9).[3] These gifts are ours as we are justified through
faith in Christ's blood, shed on the cross for us. It is justification by faith in Jesus that enables God to be a faithful God,
giving his people what he promises.

The response to justification by faith

As you, or others, grasp the extraordinary claim of justification by faith in all its fullness, it may elicit one of three
responses. It is therefore worth pondering a moment on each
of these three as a means of growing in both our discipleship
and our evangelism.

1. 'Why bother with me?'
It can feel like it is all too good to be true. People who feel
they've done something really bad in the past often feel that
God could never bother with them and forgive them. I've had
people say straight to my face that there is no hope for them
because of something they did in their past that means they
deserve hell. And in a way they are right. In fact, we all do.
But they're missing the crucial truth: God loves them, and so
God does bother with them.

   When I was trying to buy a flat for the first time, just before
exchanging contracts, the vendor pulled out of the sale. I had
already spent lots of money on solicitors' fees and surveys. I
was gutted. I felt sick to the pit of my stomach. And then one
of my close relatives heard what had happened, felt sorry for

me, and sent me a cheque for exactly the amount of money that I had already forked out.

Now why did this relative wipe out my debts? Obviously, it was because of her love for me. And it is exactly the same principle with God – though in this instance our debt is far greater, and his love is far more. However much or little we think our lives are worth, God thinks that we are precious enough to send his Son to die on a cross. He wants every one of us to be in a right relationship with him for eternity, but he has to bring us into that right relationship. He is most certainly bothered about us.

Think of King David. He was a liar, an adulterer and a murderer. You can't get much worse than that, and yet God bothered with him. God credited him as righteous through faith (Romans 4:6). David's own words are quoted by Paul and they are ones that every person trusting in Christ can know for themselves:

> Blessed are those
> whose transgressions are forgiven,
> whose sins are covered.
> Blessed is the one whose sin the Lord will never count
> against them.
> (Romans 4:7–8)

There's nothing more wonderful, nothing that more powerfully lifts all that weighs heavily on me, than knowing my sins are forgiven, covered and never to be counted against me. All because of Jesus. Justification by faith makes that possible.

2. 'Why bother being good?'

Justification by faith means there is nothing that I can do to make God love me any more, and there is nothing that I can do to make God love me any less. And yet it's strange, that as a vicar, whenever I've got an important talk to give, I make sure I get up early and have a good time with God, praying and reading the Bible. Like a good Christian boy. As I go about my day before giving the talk, I'm that little bit more vigilant that I don't look lustfully at some good-looking woman I pass on the street. Like a good Christian boy.

Now why am I like that? It is because deep down I am somehow afraid that if I am not a good Christian boy, then I will forfeit God's blessing on the talk that I'm giving. I act as though the blessing in my Christian life is based on works rather than grace. And I would wager that most of us act like this most of the time. Just do a quick self-assessment. Why do you have a quiet time? Why do you give some of your money to the church? Why are you good?

Too often, it is because we think that if we are not good, then God will either punish us and make us suffer, or else he will withhold some blessing from us. Yet God doesn't work like that. God will bless you and me – despite our sinfulness, despite our disobedience, despite our stuff-ups. If it depended on me and my works, then I would constantly lose all of God's blessings all of the time.

In Christ, God will *never* judge me for *any* of my sins (Romans 4:8). The radical thing is that as I take in the magnitude of this forgiveness, so I want God to work in me all the more, to rid sin from my life. I want to be good. I want to please God and obey him. When my heart and mind have been captivated by being justified by faith in Christ, then my motive for being good is a right one. No longer am I wanting to be good so that I won't forfeit God's blessing. Rather, I am now wanting to be good, in response to the fact that God has already blessed me.

3. 'Why bother with faith?'

Some dismiss the Christian gospel of justification by faith as lacking in credibility, because they feel faith itself is lacking in credibility. I've had people say to me, 'I wish I had your faith', but really I know that what they mean is, 'I can't believe you are bonkers enough to believe all that nonsense about rising from the dead and miracles and the second coming of Jesus.'

My answer to that is that faith is not the opposite of evidence. Nietzsche said, 'Faith is not wanting to know what is true', and Richard Dawkins declares that 'The whole point of religious faith, its strength and chief glory, is that it does not depend on rational justification',[4] but Nietzsche and Dawkins are wrong. God doesn't ask us to have faith without giving us the evidence. We do need to take a step of faith, but faith is not some random blind leap of faith. It is belief in Jesus, whom we cannot see, yet whom we can trust on the basis of reasonable, reasoned-through, thought-out evidence.

The evidence for Christianity is not like a mathematical equation, where it can be said with total certainty that $2 + 2 = 4$. Christianity cannot be proved with absolute certainty. This should not trouble us, for the majority of our beliefs in everyday life are not based upon certainty, but credibility. I am not 100% certain that my chair will hold my weight, but it is a 100% credible view, and I put my faith in it as I write this book seated at my desk. I am not 100% certain that the carrot cake my wife has just given me is poison-free, but it is a 100% credible view, and I put my faith in this view as I eat the cake, while dropping crumbs over my computer keyboard.

It is just the same with the Christian gospel. The red Lego block makes sense. It is a 100% credible view, and it is worth incorporating in 100% of life, and, personally, I put my faith in this view as I live my life on Planet Earth.

100% activation

'What gets me is that you're all so bloody confident about it all.'[5]
When I heard these words from Richard Dawkins about the faith
of Christians in Christ, it made me smile a lot, because I agree with
him that I do have a lot of confidence in my faith. But it is a fair
question to ask about, and I am always pleased to be challenged
on this as I find it incredibly encouraging and faith-building.

So what is my faith built on? What gives me confidence that
Christianity is credible? How do I measure credibility? What does
it look like?

I took a very logical and rational approach when I started
looking into Christianity (and I did so with the expectation that
I'd be able to prove it was some sort of scam). I undertook nearly
a year of research: lots of reading of both Christian and atheist
philosophy, including Dawkins, Hitchens and Flew; the
Christianity Explored course; listening to excellent Bible teaching
and Christian-versus-atheist debates; and reading rigorous
philosophy that I found in William Lane Craig's 'Reasonable
Faith' podcasts. It also included talking to my friends (and some
light mockery from them!).

Ultimately, the arguments that convinced me were simple and
factual, not spiritual and philosophical. I discovered: that Jesus
Christ was a real historical character; that he died on the cross;
and that he was seen alive again by many people, even those who
had an interest in denying that he was alive.

Surrounding this core set of facts, there were many other
arguments that convinced me and that I still find mind-blowing
today, such as how Jesus fulfilled every prophecy about him,
including his own birth and death, and the arguments of the
fine-tuning of the universe.

So what? What does all that prove, and what are the
implications? I found the answer to this question in response

to a challenge on the Christianity Explored course. If Jesus predicted his death and resurrection (the ultimate prediction?!), and it came true, then surely everything else he said must have been true?

I realized some months later that although I didn't know all the answers to every single question (and I still don't), I had full confidence in what the Bible taught, and so I decided that I must become a follower of Jesus Christ. In fact, as I delve deeper into Christian theology and apologetics through prayer, and as I research things to answer my remaining questions, I always find sound, rational and reasonable answers. This has helped develop my relationship with God.

100% credible, really? Taking the evidence into account, I would say yes, absolutely. But for those who need more persuading I would recommend talking to God about it directly.

(Chris Goff, civil servant)

100% adoration

Heavenly Father, thank you that it is credible to be a Christian.
Thank you that I can believe in Jesus through reasonable,
    reasoned-through, thought-out evidence.
Thank you for the wonder of being justified by faith.
Thank you that it doesn't depend on me.
Help me not to want to be good due to a fear of forfeiting your
    blessing.
Rather, help me to want to be good,
    in response to the fact that you have already showered your
        blessing upon me.
Thank you for the wonder of the cross,
    and that in Jesus I am protected from your wrath.

Please pour out your love into my heart by the Holy Spirit.
In Jesus' name I pray.
Amen.

3. Christianity is 100% credible

The rationale for justification by faith	The response to justification by faith
Justification by faith shows:	1) 'Why bother **with me?**'
1) God is not **fickle** *(4:1–8)*	2) 'Why bother **being good?**'
2) God does not have **favourites** *(4:9–25)*	3) 'Why bother **with faith?**'
3) God is **faithful** *(5:1–11)*	

100% application

1. Why do you want to be good?
2. When and why do you doubt your faith?
3. Why does God bother with you?
4. How is your heart warmed by meditating on the truths written about in this chapter?

Read Romans 4 – 5.

PART 2: 100% PASSION

'The problem with the devil is not his theology, but his desires.'[1] So writes the US pastor John Piper. And he's right. While part 1 of this book has included our emotions and our actions, the primary appeal has been to our intellect. In everyone, Jesus longs for an intellectual assent to the 100% gospel – a gospel which has not been emaciated through the removal of central elements, or engorged through regrettable additions. Yet intellectual assent is not enough. The devil intellectually believes the 100% gospel. His theology is correct, but his desires are catastrophic.

We can have a similar problem to the devil if our emotions remain unengaged with the gospel. What is known in the *head* must have an impact in the *heart*. Intellectual assent must lead to an impact on our emotions and desires. When we become a red Lego tower, it feels different. Of course, we will never have perfect sin-free emotions in life before death, but connecting to the 100% gospel should lead to us having a passion for God, his people and his glory.

I remember when Susannah was pregnant with our first child, Daisy. Intellectually, I knew that we were having a child. I knew this had implications for the future. Cot, buggy, baby bath, baby monitor, baby toys, and so on. Intellectually, I knew what was coming. Yet in a strange way, my emotions did not properly kick into action until the day Daisy was born. Partly, I'll be honest, this was because I was rather petrified about having a daughter. When the twenty-week scan came, and we were told that a little girl was on the way, fear was a more significant emotion than delight. Having gone to boys-only schools from the age of four, and having grown up with only a brother and no sister, it was dawning on me with all too great a realization that I didn't have a clue how little girls worked! So during the pregnancy, it was, for me, more an intellectual journey, with the emotions slow to get involved.

All that changed at 8.01 pm on 19 November 2005. This is a family book, so I'm not allowed to go into all the gory details. Suffice it to say that there were a few complications in the labour ward, and it was touch and go as to whether the doctors needed to perform an emergency caesarean on Susannah. But then, suddenly and rather hastily, Daisy decided she would make an entry into the world at a rapid pace, with the umbilical cord lassoed round her neck a couple of times. I ended up having to dive and catch my daughter to save her from landing on the hospital floor.

As I left the hospital sometime after midnight, wife and daughter in hospital bed and plastic cot respectively, I took one pace out of the building and burst into floods of tears. Good tears. Happy tears. Relieved tears. Those tears were the mark of my emotions catching up with my intellect. Suddenly I didn't just know that I had a daughter. That night I became passionate about it.

In my first couple of years as a Christian, it was a similar journey for me. Letting the emotions catch up with the intellect, as I increasingly felt and experienced the love and the joy of a relationship with Jesus. For others I know, it has been the other way round. The emotional experience has come first, and then they've needed to firm up the intellectual backbone of their Christian belief. The order doesn't matter, but the necessity of both is essential. Indeed, for every believer there needs to be a lifelong focus on both intellectual and emotional growth in our faith.

The preacher and theologian Jonathan Edwards is famous for, among other things, his treatise on 'Religious Affections'. He began the first part of this work by quoting 1 Peter 1:8: 'Though you have not seen him, you love him; and even though you do not see him now, you believe in him and are filled with an inexpressible and glorious joy.' Edwards noted that this verse was written to people who were subject to suffering and persecution, and yet they were marked by love for Christ and joy in Christ. He thus starts his book with a central hypothesis:

> Hence the proposition or doctrine, that I would raise from these words, is this:
> DOCTRINE. *True religion, in great part, consists in holy affections.*[2]

I use the word 'passion' rather than 'affections' – but the meaning is the same. As Edwards notes, not all affections or emotions or passion are necessarily from God. Some emotions can turn into emotionalism, which is unhealthy and unhelpful. Yet the danger of excessive emotionalism should never be used as a reason to cut out the emotional dimension of our faith.

As the eighteenth-century spiritual giant declares, true religion consists in holy affections. Or, as the twenty-first-century spiritual pygmy suggests, 100% Christianity encourages 100% passion.

4. CHRISTIANITY IS 100% STRUGGLE

(Romans 6 – 7)

> What shall we say, then? Shall we go on sinning, so that
> grace may increase? By no means! We are those who have
> died to sin; how can we live in it any longer? Or don't you
> know that all of us who were baptised into Christ Jesus
> were baptised into his death? We were therefore buried
> with him through baptism into death in order that, just
> as Christ was raised from the dead through the glory of
> the Father, we too may live a new life.
> (Romans 6:1–4)

I used to meet pastorally with someone who really struggled
sexually. He was a Christian, but he had found himself getting
involved in a number of one-night stands with various people
which had sometimes ended in sexual intercourse, usually due
to drinking too much alcohol. At the same time, this man
was also struggling with depression. As a result, as well as
prescribing anti-depressants, his GP also encouraged him to
visit a counsellor.

In my role as a church minister, I must admit that I found
my meetings with this man quite a challenge. Some days he
would be fairly indifferent about his night-time antics,
declaring that it was a relief that he was saved by faith in

Christ's work on the cross, and so he didn't need to worry too much about how he behaved, because God always forgave him. Other times, he would beat himself up about his actions, declaring that he was probably not really a Christian as a result of what he had done. All this wasn't helped by his trips to the counsellor, who told him that he was suffering from false guilt, and that he shouldn't feel guilty about these one-night stands because 'it's just what young people do'. In fact, so often, it was very soon after he had visited his counsellor that he slipped up again sexually.

This guy particularly struggled sexually, but for other Christians, the battle will rage strongest in different areas. For me, one of my greatest struggles is impatience, which comes to light through moments of frustrated anger. I all too easily snap at a family member or a colleague if they are not doing things in the way and at the speed that I want them to. It is a deeply ugly trait. It is born out of selfishness, and an incorrect and unattractive subconscious attitude that I think I should be at the centre of the universe. And, just like this guy with his sexual struggles, the way I respond to my struggle with impatience veers between two seemingly contrasting positions.

Sometimes I make excuses that my impatience isn't that big a problem. I almost pretend that it is not really a sin, and if it is, that God is not too fussed about it. I act as though it's not that big a deal. James Bond had a licence to kill. I give myself a licence to sin.

At other times, my impatience really gets me down, and I start to question whether I should really be a church minister at all, and even whether I have a genuine faith at all. Maybe I'm losing my salvation – or perhaps I never had it in the first place?

These two contrasting reactions to a struggle with sin – 'licence to sin' and 'losing my salvation' – are not only common to me and the guy I used to pastor, but they are also common to Paul in the letter of Romans. His teaching for struggling Roman Christians back then is just as vital for struggling Christians today.

Licence to sin? 'If my salvation is not dependent on what I do, am I free to sin?'

Paul actually asks this question twice in his letter (Romans 6:1, 15), both times immediately answering his rhetorical question with the phrase, 'By no means'. He is clear that, though our salvation is completely by grace, Christians do not have a licence to sin as much as we like, and he gives three reasons for this.

1. A new life (Romans 6:1–14)

Becoming a Christian is not just turning over a new leaf, but is a completely new life. Any baptism via full immersion is a great visual picture of this – unless I am the one doing the baptizing. The last time I baptized adults in a baptismal pool, there were about eight candidates. One guy, as soon as he had been 'dunked', sprinted out of the pool and ran straight out of the church, much to the surprise of everyone in the congregation. However, that was better than with another of the candidates, who was huge – about 6 ft 6 in height and almost the same width. With the help of someone else, I managed to lower him down into the pool, under the water, but then we weren't strong enough to lift him back up. And slowly, he started rolling over onto his front so that he was marooned, floating face down in the water, with me too weak to lift him up again. It was a complete disaster!

However, when baptism is done as it should be done, it is a brilliant picture. As the new Christian is lowered back under the water, it is a picture of his or her old life being buried and put to death. Then, as the person is brought back up out of the water, it is a demonstration that he or she has started out on a new life with Christ. As Paul writes, 'We were therefore buried with Christ through baptism into death in order that, just as [Christ] was raised from the dead through the glory of the Father, we too may live a new life' (Romans 6:4).

Becoming a Christian is not just the 'new leaf' of the additional red Lego block. It is a wholesale 100% transformation – from white Lego tower to red Lego tower. It is as radical as a new life. We are to 'count [ourselves] dead to sin but alive to God in Christ Jesus' (Romans 6:11). We are not free to sin, because we have died to sin. To sin is a total contradiction of who we are. When a caterpillar becomes a butterfly, it doesn't start trying to live like a caterpillar again. When we move jobs, we don't still go back to our old workplace each day. And as Christians, it is a total contradiction of who we are to want to sin. We have a new life.

2. A new lord (Romans 6:15–23)

Not only do we have a new life as Christians, but we also have a new lord. We are all originally part of 'Team Adam'. Adam was the first human who sinned. We follow in his line and are therefore part of his team. Yet, in dying, Jesus established a new team, 'Team Jesus', and becoming a Christian is about moving from the lordship of Adam to the lordship of Christ (Romans 5:12–21). Or again it is about moving from being slaves to sin, to being slaves to God (Romans 6:22). Our lord is Jesus. We are in a new team, with Christ in charge.

To sin is to forget what our new lord, Christ, has done for us. A while ago some tourists were visiting Notre Dame Cathedral in Paris and were looking at a painting of Jesus' death on the cross, when the bishop walked past. The bishop stopped and spoke to them. 'You know there's a story about that painting,' he said. He told the tourists about a hard, rebellious gang of teenagers, who let in new members to their gang only on the condition that they first did a dare set by the gang.

One boy wanted to join the gang, and his dare was that he had to come into the cathedral, stand in front of this painting of Jesus' crucifixion, and say three times out loud at the top of his voice, 'Jesus Christ! You died for me. And I don't give a damn.'

The boy ventured into the cathedral, stood in front of the painting, and began to shout. All he could speak out was, 'Jesus Christ! You died for me', before he broke down in tears, unable to finish the sentence. In that moment, the teenager realized what Jesus had done for him to set him free from the punishment he deserved. It melted his heart, and he gave his life to Jesus right there.

The tourists asked the bishop how he had heard the story. 'I didn't hear it,' replied the bishop. 'That boy was me.'[1]

To sin is a total forgetfulness of what Christ has done for us. It is only because of Jesus' death that we are able to be transferred from Team Adam to Team Jesus. Grasping what our new lord, Christ, has done for us is the catalyst for not wanting to sin.

3. A new love (Romans 7:1–6)
I remember at school being forced to learn Spanish. I didn't want to learn it. I was no good at it, and at the time it seemed totally irrelevant and pointless. I'd never been to Spain. In fact, I've still never been to Spain. Yet I worked hard at learning Spanish only because I had a GCSE exam in the subject and I wanted to get a good grade. If I'd been guaranteed a good

grade in my exam, I wouldn't have done an ounce of work in trying to learn the language.

This is a similar kind of dilemma to living the Christian life. Why bother learning Spanish when you're already guaranteed a good grade? It's similar to thinking, 'Why bother not sinning when I'm already guaranteed heaven?'

The only reason that my desire to speak Spanish would change is if Susannah, my wife, suddenly only spoke Spanish. If that was the case I'd suddenly start learning Spanish in record time. I'd be up late filling my brain with the language so I could communicate more with my wife than I can with my current knowledge of it, which is fairly limited. I managed to scrape an A grade in my GCSE, yet truthfully, the only two sentences in Spanish that I can still remember twenty years later are: '*Donde esta el castillo?*', which means 'Where is the castle?', and '*Dos cervezas por favor*', which translates as 'Two beers please'. As you can tell, neither of these would be a huge help in sustaining my relationship with a Spanish-speaking Susannah. Nor are they a great advert for the rigour of the GCSE examination system in the UK.

It is only the love for my now Spanish-speaking wife that would cause me to want to speak Spanish. I would want to please her, and relate well with her. Similarly, the Christian is married to Christ. Jesus is our new love. We 'belong to another, to him who was raised from the dead' (Romans 7:4). We want to please him. In fact, to sin is a violation of my relationship with Christ. It's like committing adultery. I have my new love, Christ, but I am charging off and rekindling my relationship with an old flame called 'sin'.

Martin Lloyd-Jones wrote that,

> we have to realize that we are called, in the Christian life, to a battle, not a life of ease; to a battle, to warfare, to wrestling, to a struggle.[2]

We are deluding ourselves if we think that we can live as a Christian with no struggle with sin. Christianity is a 100% struggle. There is never a time in this life when we are free from temptation. It is an ongoing battle. We need to be alert to it.

My relationship with gyms has always been rather mixed and intermittent. The best I managed was when I went to the gym at least once a week for a year. It wasn't a huge amount of use. I'd start off doing battle with a few of the machines, but after five minutes, as the excitement wore off and the pain wore on, I would migrate to the swimming pool to continue my exercise regime. The swimming pool was little bigger than a glorified paddling pool, but still, after doing ten lengths, I felt I had expended enough energy, and so headed for the jacuzzi, where I wallowed in the bubbles like a contented hippopotamus for the remainder of my allotted time.

We don't have to work to earn our relationship with Christ. Yet being a Christian is not a call to be idle. We don't lie back into Jesus like we (or at least I – I can't speak for you) lie back in a jacuzzi. We are to do battle with the sin in our lives. So when we are tempted to sin (particularly when we think it's not a big deal to sin – after all, God will forgive me), then perhaps the most powerful action we can take is to remind ourselves of our status as a Christian. In Christ, we have a new life, a new lord and a new love. Because we have a new life, sin is a contradiction of who we are. Because we have a new lord, sin is failing to recognize our new master. And because we have a new love, sin is a violation of our relationship with Jesus.

I have to be honest. So often, when the beckoning finger of temptation is luring me into sin, be it the sin of impatience I mentioned earlier, or the sin of pride or lust or greed or selfishness or whatever else, I so rarely focus on my new life, new lord and new love. Yet that is the most successful way of resisting temptation. It is little help, in the face of some sin, just to tell ourselves to change. Rather, we need to replace the wrong desires that we have with a greater desire, for something better. Being captivated again by our new life, new lord and new love is the best way to be freed from the captivations of unhelpful temptations.

As Paul introduces his section on the armour of God in his letter to the Ephesians, I love the simplicity of his advice. He writes, 'Finally, be strong in the Lord and in his mighty power' (Ephesians 6:10). Experience tells us that there are two basic mistakes Christians make. One is to become spiritually lazy. The other is not to trust the Lord. This short and concise command of Paul deals with both of those mistakes. To spiritually lazy Christians, treating Jesus like a jacuzzi to lie back in, without exerting themselves in the struggle to live a holy life, this verse says, 'Be strong.' To untrusting Christians, who run around trying to live for Jesus, being active, doing battle in their own strength, this verse says: stop charging around in your own strength, but do it 'in the Lord and in his mighty power'.

One of the only reasons my wife, Susannah, was interested in me, when we first met, was because I told her that I was a keen surfer. What I meant by this statement was that I possess a boogie board and like to head out into the waves from time to time. So I'm rather like a beached whale, or perhaps a beached hippopotamus, sprawled on a board in a wetsuit, catching a few waves while lying down. What Susannah, having grown up in Australia among rippling surf gods, thought that I meant was that I was an expert at standing on a malibu board, surfing the tube of a 10 ft breaker. By the time she realized the discrepancy between her view and the reality, it was, thankfully, too late for her to back out of our relationship. Yet the surfer, standing on a board, is a good picture of the Christian life.

Just like standing on a surfboard, life as a Christian requires us to be active. We need to be strong and stand firm. It requires effort. Yet all we need to do is stand. There is another force, the power of the Holy Spirit, carrying us forward like a wave and enabling us to live more and more as Jesus would want us to live. We are to be strong in the Lord and in his mighty power.

Losing my salvation? 'If I sin, does that mean I am not certain of my salvation?'

No matter how good a Christian surfer we are, we still sin. Our active struggle to resist sin, along with the Holy Spirit's power in our life, will not lead to a total eradication of sin. Even the great apostle Paul sinned. The struggle with sin was an ongoing, ever-present battle for him. He wrote, 'We know that the law is spiritual; but I am unspiritual, sold as a slave to sin. I do not understand what I do. For what I want to do I do not do, but what I hate I do' (Romans 7:14–15). If Paul, and we too, are supposed to be in Christ's realm (Team Jesus) with Christ as our lord, how can we still be slaves to sin (acting as though we are in Team Adam)? Does this mean we are not actually certain of our salvation after all?

The reason that there is this ongoing struggle with sin in our lives is because, while it is true that as Christians we are in Christ's realm, it is also true that, in this life, we are still in Adam's realm.[3] We live in the overlap between the two realms, and that is why we experience this struggle as Christians. Paul speaks for all Christians when he says,

> I know that nothing good lives in me, that is, in my sinful nature.
> For I have the desire to do what is good, but I cannot carry it out.

> For what I do is not the good I want to do; no, the evil I do not
> want to do – this I keep on doing.
> (Romans 7:18–19 NIV 1984)

There is a tension between our intentions and our actions. We have the desire to do what is good but we cannot carry it out.

At the moment, Daisy and Boaz are learning to swim. As a proud dad, I have to say that they are doing brilliantly. When we last went to the local swimming pool, they announced their intention to power up and down the 25-metre pool like Michael Phelps.

Yet their actions didn't quite match their intentions. They managed one length without stopping – but they were exhausted. They currently just don't have the strength and endurance to go a long distance. Rather like their dad in the gym.

Very soon, that will all have changed. Daisy and Boaz will get stronger and will be zipping up and down the pool, while their dad urges them on from the jacuzzi. For us as Christians, the change is not so rapid. Indeed, all through our earthly lives, while, God willing, we will become more Christ-like over time, we will never get to a point where we are without sin. We'll be like Daisy and Boaz right now, trying to swim many lengths of the pool. The intentions are there. We want to do it, but the actions fail. We stumble and fall into sin, because we live in this overlap. To use the language Paul uses in Romans 7, our inner being is in Christ's realm, but our sinful nature remains in Adam's realm.

If all that sounds rather discouraging, well, here's the encouragement: failing God and falling into sin does not mean that we are losing our salvation. Far from it. The difference between the 'before' and 'after' of becoming a Christian is not that before we sinned, and after we're sinless. Rather, the difference is that before becoming a Christian, sin was in character and it did not really concern us, whereas after becoming a Christian, sin becomes out of character and we don't want to sin. It causes us pain and regret when we do, not so much because we have let ourselves down, but because we want to please Christ, and we've let him down.

If, like me, you know only too well this battle and struggle with sin, then the encouragement is that this is actually a key mark of the genuine Christian believer. This is the normal Christian life. One hundred per cent struggle. The concern comes if we know nothing of this battle with sin. If the Christian life is more a breeze than a battle, then either we're not taking sin very seriously, or perhaps we're not yet a believer at all.

As I look at myself as a Christian in terms of being in Christ's realm, I realize that I am not free *to* sin. Yet, as I look at myself as a Christian still in Adam's realm, I realize that I am not free *from* sin either. This is the 100% struggle. We are not free to sin, but we are also not free from sin.

The struggle never goes away. Just like Paul, all of us who are Christians can echo the apostle's words that, 'I myself in my mind am a slave to God's law, but in the sinful nature a slave to the law of sin' (Romans 7:25b). God's law and the law of sin are in constant battle in our lives. We need to be realistic.

And yet, in the realism, we can know huge encouragement.

First, we can remember that the struggle is temporary. There is a rescue from the struggle of this life. As Paul cries out, 'What a wretched man I am! Who will rescue me from this body of death? Thanks be to God – through Jesus Christ our Lord!' (Romans 7:24–25a NIV 1984). In the future we will be rescued by Jesus from this struggle.

Second, we can remember that those who struggle are always accepted. 'Therefore, there is now no condemnation for those who are in Christ Jesus' (Romans 8:1). God looks at us in our best moments and in our worst moments, and he declares that he loves us and accepts us as we are, because Christ has paid the price of our sin. Even when we succumb to sin in our struggle, God makes his declaration of 'No condemnation' over us.

Third, we can remember that we have the Spirit helping us in the midst of the struggle with sin, for 'through Jesus Christ the law of the Spirit of life set me free from the law of sin and death' (Romans 8:2 NIV 1984). No matter what struggles we are battling with, God himself, the Almighty God, the Creator of the world, is at work in his people by his Spirit, making us more like Christ. Because of the Holy Spirit, the Christian is held on to and propelled forward on the surfboard of the Christian life. Even when we're feeling like a beached hippopotamus.

100% activation

It starts innocently enough – the quick look at page three and then listening to that voice that says it is OK to move on to the top shelf, as it is not hurting anyone. Besides, the only person who knows about it is you.

Then, late one night (and after you have had a few drinks), you fire up the computer and enter an address, and again that voice that says it is OK returns and you start watching. You feel fine about it, as the voice that says it is OK tells you that you are not hurting anyone. Besides, the only person who knows about it is you.

Eventually though, it does start to have an effect – you find it difficult to develop real, deep, meaningful relationships as you are always comparing the person you meet in real life to the person on a specific page of the latest magazine you have just bought or in the latest clip you have seen. You seem to be spending money on very short-term gratification. Any pleasurable feeling does not last long, whereas the feeling of being ashamed and embarrassed returns quickly. It also makes your relationship with God a little tricky. You are able to tell him about everything except this, because you are embarrassed/ashamed/scared of what you are doing and you would rather God didn't know about this part of your life.

So what do you do about it? How do you stop? Telling someone you trust is a good start. Also avoid going into the place where you used to buy the magazine. There any many applications available that stop you accessing certain sites on the internet. Download them and enter the site details. Don't fire up the computer if you are tired. You will start to recognize when you are most tempted to either buy a magazine or access a certain site.[4]

The hardest part is telling God about this struggle. God only wants the best for us; he is not going to disown you if you tell him what you have been doing and that you want to stop. He will help you. It is not easy but it can be done. Yes, there will be some pain; but it is worth it, as the end result is that you feel much better about yourself, relationships become more real, you have more money, and your relationship with God is so much better. (Jeremy Smith, IT consultant)

100% adoration

Lord God, thank you for the reminder that a struggle with sin is
    the normal experience for the Christian.
Forgive me, Lord, where I have got too comfortable with sin.
Help me battle it in your strength.

Help me keep going in the struggle,
> living for you in the new life of the Spirit.

Thank you for the Lord Jesus – for his death for me
> and that one day he will rescue me from this body
>> of death that I am in.

Thank you that in Jesus there is no condemnation.

In his name I pray.

Amen.

4. Christianity is 100% struggle

Licence to sin?

'If my salvation is not dependent on what I do, am I free to sin?'

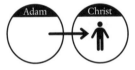

1) A new **life** *(6:1–14)*
2) A new **lord** *(6:15–23)*
3) A new **love** *(7:1–6)*

Losing my salvation?

'If I sin, does that mean I am not certain of my salvation?'

1) The struggle is **temporary** *(7:24–25)*
2) The struggler is **accepted** *(8:1)*
3) The struggler has **the Spirit** *(8:2)*

100% application

1. What are the biggest struggles with sin that you face at the moment?
2. You have a new life, a new lord, a new love. How does that make you feel?
3. What brings you comfort and strength in the midst of your struggle with sin?

4. How will you remember in your head and in your heart
   that there is 'no condemnation for those who are in
   Christ Jesus' (Romans 8:1)?

Read Romans 6 – 7.

5. CHRISTIANITY IS 100% SPIRIT-EMPOWERED

(Romans 8)

> Those who are led by the Spirit of God are [children] of
> God. For you did not receive a spirit that makes you a slave
> again to fear, but you received the Spirit of adoption. And
> by him we cry, *'Abba*, Father.' The Spirit himself testifies
> with our spirit that we are God's children.
> (Romans 8:14–16 NIV 1984)

If, as many commentators suggest, the book of Romans is the
Himalayas of the New Testament, with chapter 8 of the letter
as its Everest, then one key reason for this grandiose declaration is because of the person who is mentioned nineteen
times in the chapter. That person is the third person of the
Trinity, the Holy Spirit.

When I worked at All Souls, Langham Place, right next to
the number one shopping street in London, each year we would
have the excitement of the nearby Oxford Street Christmas
lights being switched on by some illuminating celebrity. The
idea was that you looked at the unlit Christmas decorations and
then everyone would start cooing with pleasure at the beautiful
lights when they started shining in the night's sky.

However, one year at All Souls we had the added spectacle,
in partnership with the BBC next door, of a ceremony when

the new floodlights were turned on to illuminate the church building. On this occasion everyone also cooed, but there was a difference. People were cooing not because they were looking at the lights that had been turned on, but because they were looking at the church that was newly visible in the dark.

I give this aside about lights to make the point that it is certainly true, as others have pointed out before me, that the Holy Spirit has a ministry more akin to that of a floodlight than a Christmas light.[1] The main role of the Holy Spirit is that he points us to someone else – Jesus. More than focusing on himself, the Holy Spirit lights up Jesus. He is not like a Christmas light, wanting the focus to be on himself. This means that the best test of a Spirit-filled church is not what the church is saying about the Holy Spirit. Rather, the best test is what the church is saying about Jesus. In fact, in the first seven chapters of Romans, the Holy Spirit is only mentioned twice (Romans 5:5; 7:6). As Professor Gordon Fee, the Pentecostal theologian, writes, 'The Spirit is not *the* center for Paul – Christ is, ever and always – but the Spirit stands close to the center, making Christ known and empowering all genuinely Christian life and experience.'[2]

The floodlight ministry of the Spirit is undoubtedly true, but it shouldn't be used as an excuse to marginalize and ignore the work of the Holy Spirit. This happens with some more conservative Christians, often subconsciously in opposition to the excesses of the charismatic movement. I have unconsciously been guilty of this. In the first book I wrote, *Working without Wilting*, it was not until I had submitted the complete manuscript and had it pointed out to me by two readers (Mark Greene and my mother, as it happens), that I realized I had only mentioned the Holy Spirit twice in a 200-page book. I remedied that immediately.

Fee states that the Spirit is responsible for 'empowering all genuinely Christian life and experience', and it is that fact that is minimised by some Christians. One hundred per cent Christianity must mean being 100% Spirit-empowered. After all, every single person who is in Christ is indwelt by the Spirit. It is not just particularly spiritual Christians, or Christians with certain specific gifts, who have the Spirit. As Paul notes, 'If anyone does not have the Spirit of Christ, [that person] does not belong to Christ' (Romans 8:9b). Furthermore, the Spirit is not a liquid that is poured into the Christian. God doesn't decide to pour two-thirds of a bottle of Holy Spirit into one believer, but only one-third into someone else. The Spirit is not an inanimate liquid, but an animate person. We either have him indwelling in us 100%, if we're a Christian, or we have him 0%, if we are not yet a Christian.

This means that all Christians are Spirit-filled Christians. There is no other type of Christian. Of course, as John Stott writes, 'There may be many further and richer experiences of the Spirit, and many fresh anointings of the Spirit for special tasks, but the personal indwelling of the Spirit is every believer's privilege from the beginning. To know Christ and to have the Spirit are one.'[3] Famously and crucially, Paul's exhortation to the Ephesians ('Be filled with the Spirit', Ephesians 5:18b) should literally be translated, 'Go on being filled with the Spirit'. We are actively to desire subsequent experiences of being filled by the Holy Spirit. These fillings are not about being topped up with the Spirit because we leak (again – he is not some inanimate liquid). Being filled with the Spirit is about letting him fill more and more of our lives with his love and power and influence.

When we recognize the role of the Spirit in our lives as disciples, when we don't ignore him and marginalize him, but actively look to go on being filled with the Spirit so that he empowers our Christian life and experience, then there are at least five positive outworkings.

1. Relief at the freedom (Romans 8:1–4)

When the TV presenter Michael Aspel was interviewed by the *Independent* newspaper, he talked about the seven children he had by three broken marriages. Despite the joy of the children, he spoke about this as a failure, declaring that he was very disappointed with himself. He regretted a lot of things that had happened. He summarized this by saying, 'It's . . . agonising because there is no way you can absolve it.'[4] This is perhaps the biggest struggle for those who are not yet Christians. They have no-one to forgive them and absolve them for all that they have done wrong.

It is so different for Christians. We can say with confidence that all our sin and guilt has been absolved. We face no condemnation, because Jesus was condemned in our place. God sent 'his own Son in the likeness of sinful [humanity] to be a sin offering. And so he condemned sin in sinful [humanity]' (Romans 8:3 NIV 1984). This is one of the most freeing experiences in life, and it is a work of the Spirit to know this freedom – 'through Christ Jesus the law of the Spirit of life set me free from the law of sin and death' (Romans 8:2 NIV 1984). There is such relief in experiencing this liberation.

Supremely, the freedom that the Spirit gives us is a freedom to live life as it is meant to be lived (Romans 8:4). He enables us to live holy lives that look to fulfil God's moral law. This is what God promised through the Old Testament prophets. Through Ezekiel, God promised, 'I will put my Spirit in you' (Ezekiel 36:27), and through Jeremiah, he declared, 'I will put my law in their minds and write it on their hearts' (Jeremiah 31:33).

Some people love long walks. I am not one of them – give me a short walk or no walk any day of the week. But the few times I have been forced into going for a long trek, the part I have most enjoyed is the bit just after lunch. In the morning, as you trudge along, all your food is on your back, in your backpack. It is a burden. It weighs you down. But when you stop for lunch, you eat and drink all the things that you were carrying. No longer are they external; they are now internal. Suddenly the very things that were a burden to you are firing you up, energizing you and helping you to keep going.

Similarly, the Holy Spirit takes God's law from being an external code of rules that we don't really like and certainly can't keep, and puts his law in our minds and writes it on our hearts. We don't suddenly become perfect as Christians, but we gain freedom to live life as it is meant to be lived. Jesus declared that life with him was an abundant life in all its fullness (John 10:10), and Irenaeus, the second-century bishop, was no doubt thinking of what Jesus said when he wrote that 'the glory of God is a human being fully alive'.[5] Too often in our Christian discipleship, we can slip into a mode of operation that is more about external rule-keeping than living an abundant life to the glory of God out of the overflow of a heart transformed by the Spirit of God. When we find ourselves reverting to rule-keeping, we need to cry out again to our heavenly Father that he might again work in us by his Spirit who gives us the freedom to be fully alive.

2. Power for the fight (Romans 8:5–13)

A few years ago, we had a mouse infestation in our flat. It was not a pleasant experience. The property next door had been deserted for nine months and the mice had been breeding (like rabbits). Then the pneumatic drills came in to gut the place and turn it into four deluxe apartments. As soon as the drills came in, the mice came out. They left the property next door and came into ours.

Eventually we were so overrun that we had to evacuate for five weeks while Camden council's finest rodent destroyers came to the rescue. In the build-up to our evacuation, I became something of an expert at catching mice. Once I had psychoanalysed the mice, worked out how they operated and what they liked (chocolate muffins, for the record), I managed to catch them with great regularity. My record on one snap trap was seven in thirty-six hours.

Sometimes the mouse was killed straight away, but sometimes (apologies for the gruesome information) it took a while to die because it was caught in the trap just by its tail or its leg. A friend was horrified when he discovered that I generally finished them off by popping them into a plastic bag and whacking them over the head with a hammer. He was appalled at my barbarism – until his flat was also overrun with mice, and he was forced to admit the necessity of my actions!

As Christians, our battle with sin is similar to my battle with the mice. Some sin is killed straight away, but most sin wriggles and writhes and tries to bite back at us for quite some time. It will die, but not straight away. In the past, when we start out as Christians, the *penalty* of sin is dealt with (Romans 8:1). In the future, after death, or when Jesus returns, the *presence* of sin will be totally removed (Romans 8:11). But it is in the present that the *power* of sin is being dealt with, sometimes killed straight away, sometimes wriggling and writhing over time. This power of sin is dealt with by the power of the Holy Spirit in our lives: 'If you live according to the sinful nature, you will die; but if by the Spirit you put to death the misdeeds of the body, you will live' (Romans 8:13 NIV 1984).

If we minimize the role of the Spirit in our lives, then the danger is that we end up thinking that any change in our lives is down to our own efforts. We adopt a New Year's resolution mentality, striving to keep the latest new goal for our life. Yet we soon discover that we end up breaking this resolution again and again and again. What we all need is a power at work inside us, but which comes from outside us. This is the only way that real, lasting change is going to take place. It requires not just our resolution, but rather a revolution brought about by the Spirit of God. It is the Holy Spirit that provides the power for change in our lives.

Perhaps my favourite prayer in the entire Bible is Paul's prayer for power in Ephesians 3:14–21. Three times in these verses, Paul asks God to strengthen the Ephesians with power. Earlier in the letter, in a previous prayer, he reminds the Ephesians, and us, that God's power at work in us is the same force that raised Jesus from the dead (Ephesians 1:19–20). The strength of God's power is seen in the resurrection, but the source of it in our lives is mediated to us through the work of his Spirit. Paul says, 'I pray that out of [God's] glorious riches he may strengthen you with power through his Spirit in your inner being' (Ephesians 3:16).

This is a prayer for the Christian to be filled with the Spirit. The problem is that while all Christians will agree that we need to go on being filled with the Spirit (Ephesians 5:18), there is disagreement on what this looks like in practice. The conservative will tend to want to tie the filling of the Spirit of God so exactly with the Word of God that the only means of being filled with the Spirit is seen to be when the Bible is open and a sermon that we are listening to is impacting our lives. Similarly the charismatic will tend to tie the filling of the Spirit to times of prayer ministry, as someone is praying for the Spirit to work in our lives.

Both are in danger of having too narrow a view. Paul continues the prayer by asking for God to strengthen the Ephesians 'with power through his Spirit in your inner being, so that *Christ may dwell in your hearts* through faith' (Ephesians 3:16–17, my italics). The result of being filled with the Spirit will always be that more and more, we become places where Christ dwells and feels comfortable. The word 'dwell' in Paul's prayer is a really strong word that is all about taking up residence and settling down and making a home.

We own a house in Pembrokeshire where we go for all our holidays. It's in an amazing location, near some spectacular beaches. Friends who have never been to the house refer to it as our 'cottage' in Wales, but when they do this they fall foul of the Trade Descriptions Act. Friends who have actually been there never make that mistake, because the house is not a picturesque cottage, but a neglected semi-detached ex-council bungalow. When we bought it, it looked ugly on the inside as well as the outside.

But, over the years, we have been making the neglected semi-detached bungalow nice on the inside. We've pulled up carpets that smell of cat pee and put down cat-pee-free new ones. We've sanded the floors. We've painted the walls. With the substantial help of a friend who is good at DIY, we've pulled out the modern brick fireplace and put in a wood-burning stove. More and more, the house has become somewhere we can dwell, somewhere we can feel comfortable when we go on holiday.

Similarly, the result of being filled with the Spirit is that more and more, even if we look as ugly as our house does on the outside, we are becoming a place where Jesus Christ feels comfortable, somewhere he can dwell because we are as he wants us to be. So ecstatic utterances and physical manifestations are not essential to being filled with the Spirit, but neither can the Spirit's work be confined to when the Bible is physically open. We are filled with the Spirit whenever we become a place where Christ can dwell more comfortably. That may be as a result of a sermon or a time of prayer ministry, or a song that is sung, or as we take communion, or as we read and pray in the quiet of our rooms, or through a conversation with a friend or through a hundred other ways.

We have all probably been in churches where, five minutes after the sermon, the final song concluded, the service is over and everyone is sipping on a coffee and talking about the latest travails of their favourite sports team. This is a tragedy. The time straight after the Word is preached is the perfect opportunity for the Word to be prayed in during a time of prayer ministry where the body of Christ can pray for one another, asking the Spirit to continue to be at work in power, causing change in our lives and breaking the power of sin so that we might become more like Christ. More 'charismatic' churches have often helpfully led the way here.

That struggle with the power of sin in our lives can be an ongoing battle, but the Spirit helps us in it. Sometimes, rather like my hammer with the mice, the Spirit works in power to bring a significant breakthrough in causing death to some particular sin or struggle in an individual's life. As I think over the last couple of years, I can think of individuals who have had breakthroughs in their lives in areas such as desiring to resist internet porn, changed attitudes towards difficult colleagues, being able to forgive parents, and knowing release from demonic oppression. All of these came as a result of praying that the Holy Spirit might work in power to bring the teaching of God's Word into reality in their lives.

Take George. A young guy, he had a huge problem with swearing. Whenever he got angry, a torrent of crude and blasphemous words would come out of his mouth. It had got

him into trouble at school and with his family. He had had to
change schools. His parents were despairing. George longed
for change, but the problem would not disappear. In fact, it
just got bigger. Whenever he got wound up, he didn't seem
to have the power to control his tongue. Yet one day someone
prayed with him – that God's Spirit would work in power to
bring about change in this area. He (and his parents!) looks
back on that day as the decisive breakthrough in that area
of his life.

Either way, whether the Spirit brings decisive breakthrough
or ongoing help in the struggle with sin, it is by the power of
the Spirit that we 'put to death the misdeeds of the body'
(Romans 8:13). And either way, if we minimize and sideline
the work of the Spirit, we are doing a disservice to Christ's
desire to dwell more fully in our lives.

3. Intimacy with the Father (Romans 8:14–17)

If my favourite prayer in the Bible is in Ephesians 3, then my
favourite Greek word (and I know very few) is the word *monai*.
It only appears twice in the whole of the New Testament.
Both of its appearances are in John 14 as Jesus speaks to the
disciples during the last supper on the night before he goes to
the cross. Both of the appearances bring huge comfort. The
first appearance is when Jesus says, 'In my Father's house there
are many dwelling-places [*monai*]' (John 14:2 NRSV). Christians
will, after death, dwell with the Father and the Son in heaven.
In the second appearance Jesus says, 'Those who love me
will keep my word, and my Father will love them, and we will
come to them and make our home [*monai*] with them' (John
14:23 NRSV). The huge comfort is that not only in the future
will our dwelling place be with the Father and the Son in

heaven, but also in the present, the Father and the Son, through the Spirit, make their dwelling place with each Christian here on earth so that we can know our God better.

Christianity is not just about our legal standing; it is also about our relational standing. The supreme wonder of being a Christian is not actually our justification, though that is so central to the first chapters of Romans. The supreme wonder is that, as a result of being justified, we can be declared children of God because we have received the 'Spirit of adoption' (Romans 8:15).

As J. I. Packer declares in his most celebrated book, *Knowing God*, 'adoption is *the highest privilege that the gospel offers:* higher even than justification'.[6] God doesn't want us just knowing the fact that we are God's children; he wants us to experience and savour and delight in the amazing intimacy that we have been given with our Father. That is why the Spirit has been sent: 'The Spirit himself testifies with our spirit that we are God's children' (Romans 8:16).[7]

I don't think there is one particular feeling that we have as the Spirit helps us experience this intimacy with our Father. What we feel also varies depending on how God has wired each one of us. My wife, Susannah, will regularly weep when she feels joy at God being her heavenly Father and how he is working in the world and in her life. I rarely weep (except at the birth of children and while watching chick flicks). God isn't concerned about whether Susannah and I have identical feelings. Rather, his primary concern is that we both have a real, deepening relationship with him as Father. As Graham Beynon writes, intimacy with our heavenly Father 'isn't something you sit and feel; it's a relationship you live in'.[8]

When my Iraqi friend speaks to his dad in his mother tongue, he uses the word 'Abba'. It's the word Jesus himself used too. In the Garden of Gethsemane, as he prayed to God on the night before his crucifixion, he prayed 'Abba, Father' (Mark 14:36). Jesus has this unique, intimate child–parent relationship with the Father, and yet he says in the Sermon on the Mount that we too should experience such a relationship with the Father – 'Our Father in heaven' (Matthew 6:9, my italics).

I remember a friend of mine telling me about going to visit an orphanage in South Africa where his twin sister was working. He said the most shocking thing about it was that the orphanage was totally quiet. Hundreds of children, but no noise.

Russell Moore says the same thing in his book, Adopted for Life, which describes how he and his wife adopted two Russian boys to be their sons:

> Of all the disturbing aspects of the orphanage in which we found our boys, one stands out above all the others in its horror. It was quiet. The place was filled with an eerie silence . . . despite the fact that there were cribs full of babies in every room. If you listened intently enough, you could hear the sound of gentle rocking – as babies rocked themselves back and forth in their beds. They didn't cry because no one responded to their cries. So they stopped crying. That's dehumanizing in its horror.[9]

While Moore and his wife were in Russia, they would visit the two boys in preparation for adopting them. However, they then had to return home to the USA to sort out all the admin and paperwork, before flying to Russia again to take the children home with them. Moore says that leaving the orphanage to go home to the USA for that first time without the boys was one of the hardest things he has ever had to do. As they walked out of the room to leave, they could hear one of them 'calling out for us and falling down in his crib, convulsing in tears'.[10] That cry in the silence was a deeply painful moment, but it was also a glorious breakthrough. It was the first time he or his wife had ever heard one of the boys cry. Russell Moore comments about that first cry: 'it was because, for whatever reason, he seemed to think he'd be heard and, for whatever reason, he no longer liked the prospect of being alone in the dark.'[11]

What happened with that boy is similar to what happens when the Spirit is at work in you or me. The Holy Spirit enables me to know and experience that my heavenly Father is there, and that I am his adopted child. No longer am I resigned to the silence, but I can cry out from the cot of my life to the one who is for me and who loves me.[12]

Of course, whether we are an orphan or come from the most stable family background imaginable, every earthly father will have failed in some way. Yet, whatever the state of our relationship with our own earthly father, through the work of the Holy Spirit we can begin to experience intimacy with a perfect heavenly Father.

The Holy Spirit helps us to live in the light of our acceptance rather than our rejection. So often, we can find ourselves defining who we are by how we've been rejected – whether that rejection has come from our family, or a spouse, or in a job or in a church, whether that rejection has come while growing up or as an adult. Yet the contrast that Paul draws is between fear or adoption: 'you did not receive a spirit that makes you a slave again to fear, but you received the Spirit of adoption' (Romans 8:15 NIV 1984). If we have ever doubted whether God really loves us, we need doubt no longer. We are as loved and welcomed and accepted by God as Jesus is himself.

The Holy Spirit also helps us to live in the light of the future rather than the past. Our past need not define us. All of us have baggage from the past. Things we regret and have done wrong.

We all have ways that we have been hurt by others, sometimes deep hurts. There is of course an important place for Christian counselling, but the most powerful way to deal with all our baggage is to let the Holy Spirit work in us and change us so that we start defining ourselves, not by what has happened in the past, nor even by who we are and what we do in the present, but in the light of what we one day will be in the future. For, 'if we are children, then we are heirs – heirs of God and co-heirs with Christ, if indeed we share in his sufferings in order that we may also share in his glory' (Romans 8:17).

There will be sufferings now due to our own sin, other people's sin, and due to living in a world that is out of kilter with God. However, the amazing truth is that in Christ, the Spirit helps us lift our eyes to what we will be. Everything that Christ inherits, we will inherit in Christ too. God will no more stop loving us than he will stop loving Jesus. This is not a fostering arrangement where he can send me packing if I misbehave. This is adoption. It's permanent. An eternity of being loved by the Father.

This intimacy with the Father is not the privilege of a select few. Paul is describing an experience that is possible for all believers. But we all experience this intimacy to different degrees. It is therefore right for each one of us to continue to ask that the Spirit might fill us more and more so that we might relate to our Abba Father with greater and greater intimacy.

4. Expectancy about the future (Romans 8:18–25)

We can experience great intimacy with the Father now, but we can look forward to a far greater level of intimacy when we are in heaven. Another result of the Holy Spirit at work in us is that he gives us the right level of expectancy. There is a huge tension between what we experience 'now' and what we experience 'not yet'. This Everest chapter, Romans 8, is full of talk of the Holy Spirit, but it is also full of talk about groaning. The whole creation (v. 22), Christians (v. 23) and even the Holy Spirit (v. 26) are all groaning – looking forwards to a future free from struggle and suffering.

Recently, there were two male Dutch TV presenters who volunteered to experience the pain of childbirth. One of them, before the electrodes were attached to his tummy to simulate labour pains, said to camera, 'According to women, childbirth is the worst kind of pain there is. But you know, according to men, women exaggerate everything.' However, his bravado quickly disappeared as the experiment got underway, and there is YouTube footage of the two blokes moaning and groaning, and then screaming and kicking their legs in absolute agony.[13]

Yet the Bible says the groaning of the whole creation is like that: 'groaning as in the pains of childbirth' (Romans 8:22). This world is expectant, longing for an eternal future no longer out of kilter with its Creator. And it is the same for us all as individuals. In our lives there will be times when the pain just seems unbearable – so bad that we can hardly describe it. And in those times, we need to hold on to the wonder of the future.

There is so much that we wait patiently for, not least the redemption of both our bodies and the whole of creation. Yet there is a danger that we so overemphasize this call to be patient that we fall into apathy, pessimism and a belief that God cannot and will not change things in the here and now.

The reality is that as Christians we have 'the firstfruits of the Spirit' (Romans 8:23). The firstfruits were the first part of the crops which were harvested. They acted as a pledge that the complete harvest would appear at some point in the future. Elsewhere, Paul uses a metaphor from the financial world rather than the farming world (see 2 Corinthians 1:22; 5:5; Ephesians 1:14). Until recent times this word was translated 'guarantee', but it is now clear that it is more accurate to translate it as 'deposit'.

Many of us who have been involved in the purchase or sale of a house will know only too well the difference between a bare guarantee and a guarantee accompanied by a deposit. For example, Susannah and I have caused pain to others by putting an offer on a house, only to remove that guarantee before actually paying a deposit when we learned from the survey about structural problems with the house.

The Holy Spirit is not just a guarantee of what is to come in the future. He is also the firstfruits, a deposit in the here and now. He is a foretaste, as well as an assurance, of what is to come. The Holy Spirit brings a portion of the 'not yet' of God's blessing, reign and rule into the now.

We cannot demand God's intervention. We cannot attempt to force him into action. Yet we can be expectant. Take the whole area of praying for healing. We can't guarantee healing in an individual's life, but we can pray for it. Not with apathy, expecting it to make no difference, but with expectation that the Holy Spirit may choose to bring a portion of the not-yet into the now, and bring healing into an individual's life. Of course, it is true that the person who is healed now will get sick again at some point. He or she will die. That's why the greatest news about having the Spirit is that we can, with total certainty, be expectant about the long-term eternal future: 'the redemption of our bodies' (Romans 8:23). But we can have some expectancy in this life too.

Or take the area of social transformation. Jesus encouraged us to pray for the Father's kingdom to come 'on earth as it is in heaven'(Matthew 6:10). That is not merely a prayer for Christ to return, or merely a prayer for evangelistic endeavours. Of course it must include both of these, but it is also a prayer that an increased amount of God's rule will be at work in some part of God's earth in the present.

I think of Paul Cowley. Once he was a gang member and, eventually, was given a prison sentence. After Paul encountered Christ through an Alpha course in 1994, he began to go back into prison in order to run Alpha there. He went on to start an organization to care for ex-offenders. Hundreds of men and women have now been placed in churches through the ministry of Caring for Ex-Offenders. He continued by setting up a homeless project, a course for those wrestling with addiction, and another for people struggling with depression. These projects have now grown to be the William Wilberforce Trust, having a significant impact in confronting poverty and injustice and caring for those in need. Under Paul's leadership, Alpha in prisons has spread to 75% of the prisons in the UK, and eighty-one countries around the world. Over 100,000 men and women have done Alpha in UK prisons alone and thousands have come to faith in Jesus Christ.

I think of Lavinia Brennan. She's just twenty-six, yet, with a friend, she has set up a fashion label which has seen the Duchess of Cambridge wearing her dresses. However, this isn't a normal fashion company. Those involved in the production process of the clothes include women in India who have been freed from being trafficked as sex slaves. Because of Lavinia's passion for Jesus, she has developed a passion for people, whatever their background and situation. She has developed a passion for justice.

Both Paul and Lavinia have been involved in godly risk-taking. They have stepped out in faith, expectant that amazing things can be done in God's name and for God's glory because

God's Spirit is at work actively empowering and enabling their vision. Of course, patience and realism are essential, but they should not exist at the expense of expectancy. The Holy Spirit creates in us a belief that God is on the move in the present.

5. Honesty over the failures (Romans 8:26–27)

While we can be expectant at what the Holy Spirit might do in us and through us, above all we need the Spirit to be at work in our lives because we are not sorted. We need help, and 'the Spirit helps us in our weakness' (v. 26a). We are ignorant, not knowing what to pray for, and 'the Spirit himself intercedes for us with groans that words cannot express' (v. 26b). The Holy Spirit works in us in the midst of our struggles and groans and failures.

If we don't acknowledge the role of the Spirit in our daily discipleship, then one of two problems surface. In the good times, when all is well, we get too puffed up and pleased with our own abilities. In the bad times, when we have struggles or disappointments, we get too pulled down and feel inadequate and helpless. Neither situation is helpful. Acknowledging the role of the Spirit in 'empowering all genuinely Christian life and experience'[14] enables us to be thankful to him in the good times, and honest when a difficult time comes. When things are tough, rather than seeking to maintain a stiff upper lip when inside we are falling apart, we can ask God's Spirit to help us and heal us.

Church should be like a hospital in the most traditional sense of the word. It should be a place of hospitality and restoration, where a community of sinners gather together and help each other to be restored to fullness when we are sick from our own sin, or from the sin of others. One reason that this sometimes does not take place is if there is little recognition of the work of the Spirit. He helps us in our weakness. He allows us to be honest to one another about our failures, and we are all the better for it.

Freedom. Power. Intimacy. Expectancy. Honesty. It is the Holy Spirit, at work in all followers of Jesus, who enables the growth of these highly prized qualities. Yet we are not devoid of responsibility. Supremely, the question you need to ask yourself is not: 'How much of the Spirit do I have?'. Rather, the question is: 'How much of me does the Spirit have?' Have you, and I, given him full rein to work in our lives?

100% activation

When I became a Christian nine years ago, the verse in Romans 8:15 which says that as Christians we have received the Spirit of adoption was hard for me to come to terms with. I hated the idea of being adopted by God. I felt adoption meant people could do anything they wanted to you, because they hadn't given birth to you and therefore could detach themselves from any feelings towards you.

This is my own personal experience of adoption.

I was given up by my birth parents at six months old and then at the age of twelve adopted by a family I had been with since I was nine months. While I was in their care, I was shown no love and treated to many forms of physical, emotional, mental and sexual abuse. When I finally left them at sixteen, I had lost all trust in people and was angry with the world for all I had been through.

As a Christian, although I loved God and was thankful for all he had saved me from, I still had a lot of feelings of resentment towards him. I never trusted God to be my Father, or to have a hope-filled future in store for me. I blamed him for not protecting me. One day I invited the Holy Spirit into that area of my life, and things changed for me. I started to feel things that I wasn't able to feel before. I felt love towards people. I wasn't angry any more and I was able to see things that had happened in my life in a new way. I no longer blamed my adopted parents for everything that was wrong with my life. I was also able to see that God had been with me through all the difficult times, and every tear I wept he could match.

After going through a lot of healing and many prayer sessions, I decided that it was time for me to forgive my adopted parents for all that had happened. When I gave my life to Christ, I had been forgiven for so many things that I had done and therefore I needed to forgive those who had done wrong to me.

So after fourteen years of no contact, I was able to have a phone conversation with my adoptive mother. I was able to tell her that I forgave her and loved her, and then I also asked for her forgiveness for anything that she and her husband thought I had done wrong. Her reply was that it would take a long time to forgive me. I knew at that moment that the Holy Spirit truly lived in me as my response to her was that I understood and that she could take her time.

After I forgave my family, I felt such freedom and relief. I was able to let go of every bad feeling I had felt towards my adoptive parents. Instead I was left with feelings of sadness and pity towards them. When the Spirit works in us to help us become more like Christ, we begin to see people through his eyes. I was able to understand all the pain they had gone through in their own lives and how they also had been let down by their own parents. They didn't know how to love as they had never been shown love.

I still have no contact with them, but I no longer feel alone. When I was adopted by God, I was also adopted into his family, and I have finally accepted that I am a part of that.

(Nat Lewington, nanny)

100% adoration

Holy Spirit, thank you that you dwell in every single person
    who trusts in the Lord Jesus.
Thank you that you remind me of the freedom I have from the
    law of sin and death,
    and the freedom I have to live life as it is meant to be lived.
Thank you for giving me power for my fight with sin.
Thank you for the amazing intimacy that I can experience with
    my Father in heaven.
Please grow that intimacy in me.
Thank you that I can be expectant – supremely about the
    eternal future,
    but also that you are at work in the here and now,
    bringing a portion of the not-yet into the now.
Thank you that you groan for me and with me in the midst
    of my groaning.
May my local church be a place where we can be honest
    with one another about our groans,
    and come to you for help and restoration.
Thank you that you point me to Jesus.
In Jesus' name.
Amen.

5. Christianity is 100% Spirit-empowered

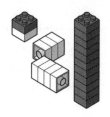

Five benefits of letting the Spirit empower
our Christian life and experience...

1) Relief at the **freedom** *(8:1–4)*
2) Power for the **fight** *(8:5–13)*
3) Intimacy with the **father** *(8:14–17)*
4) Expectancy about the **future** *(8:18–25)*
5) Honesty in the **family** *(8:26–27)*

100% application

1. How much of you does the Spirit have? Have you given
   him full rein to work in your life?
2. What will help you to live in the light of your acceptance
   rather than your rejection? And what will help you to
   live in the light of the future rather than the past?
3. How does it make you feel that God will no more stop
   loving you than he will stop loving Jesus?
4. What is the level of your expectancy about how God
   might work in your life by his Spirit? Is it too low, or
   too high?

Read Romans 8.

6. CHRISTIANITY IS 100% SATISFACTION

(Romans 5, 8)

> I am convinced that neither death nor life, neither angels
> nor demons, neither the present nor the future, nor any
> powers, neither height nor depth, nor anything else in all
> creation, will be able to separate us from the love of God
> that is in Christ Jesus our Lord.
>
> (Romans 8:38–39)

Over the last decade, Tim has been made redundant a few
times, he's been seriously ill, people dear to him have let him
down. As a result, when I met up with him, he had given up
on God. He had stopped going to church, had put away his
Bible, and stopped praying. He felt that Jesus wasn't matching
up with what Tim had expected of him. He'd become completely dissatisfied with Jesus. To take the Lego analogy, Tim
had remained a white Lego tower with a red block of the
gospel attached. When the hugely difficult and testing times
had come, after a while, he just pulled the red block off and
threw it in the bin.

It's not just Tim. In the previous year since writing this, I
can think of conversations I have had with individuals about
a whole range of personal challenges:

- The unemployed person who can't get a job
- The employed person who hates his job
- The unmarried person desperately lonely
- The married person achingly lonely within marriage
- The person struggling with same-sex attraction
- The person who has a life-threatening illness
- The person being mocked for his faith
- The person who has been accused of a crime and then been sent to prison

Such a variety of different challenges – yet all of the conversations with these different individuals were united by the common theme of a search for satisfaction and contentment in the lows of life as well as the highs.

While a more charismatic Christianity is useful in teaching us not to marginalise the role of the Spirit in the life of the believer, one of the most beneficial things with a more conservative Christianity is in encouraging Christians to know satisfaction in our faith, even in the hard times. Perhaps a key critique of a more charismatic Christianity is the lack of satisfaction and contentment that exists among believers when there is a discrepancy in life between what they expect and what they actually experience. Recognizing that as Christians we are 100% Spirit-empowered does not mean that we will be cruising along in life, 10 ft above every care and concern and complication.

Placing a right emphasis on the Holy Spirit will lead to greater freedom, power, intimacy, expectancy and honesty in our day-to-day walk with Jesus. Yet, if we have a wrong understanding of what it means to be empowered by the Spirit, we will feel huge levels of dissatisfaction and discontentment whenever we struggle or suffer. And there's no getting round it – we will suffer! For many reading this book, struggle and suffering is a live issue right now.

Jesus was full of the Spirit, but that did not mean that he could bypass the cross to get to the resurrection. That's how it was for Jesus, and that's how it is for us. The Holy Spirit doesn't enable us to bypass the struggles and sufferings of this life. If we think he does, then we will never know satisfaction in Christ.

I'll admit that satisfaction is a huge issue for me. When we moved back to London after living in Oxford for two years, we rented a flat in Clapham. Lo and behold, our next-door neighbour was someone I had been at school with. My family lived in our flat covering two floors – ground floor and basement. He owned the five-floor house next door. It really grated. Every time I walked past his house, I'd look enviously through the windows at the beautiful furniture and all the amazing mod cons. Every time, I'd think of how I had been just as successful as him at school. I was full of discontentment. It was totally ridiculous, but it's the honest truth.

And that is not the only area where I display dissatisfaction with life. So often, I think that I will be satisfied in the future if I'm living in a bigger house, or if my dodgy asymmetric vocal cord is sorted, or if I'm the head pastor of a church. I'm always thinking that I will be happy if such-and-such happens, rather than being happy in the present, whatever the circumstances. The apostle Paul may have 'learned to be content whatever the circumstances' (Philippians 4:11), but I find it a struggle – even though in reality I have so much.

The test is how we respond when we find ourselves dissatisfied and discontent with life and with God. The danger in more charismatic circles is that we look wider in search of new things to help us get satisfaction. This isn't just the problem in extreme Pentecostal settings, like Believe TV, which a few years ago faced investigations after a televangelist informed viewers that if they used a certain olive oil soap they would be cured of cancer.[1] It is the problem every time someone looks beyond God to something new in search of satisfaction.

Perhaps it is the person expecting to find an ideal spouse, but experiencing the frustration of remaining single. As a result of the gap between expectation and experience, he decides to head back to his old way of life and starts dating and then gets married to a person who isn't a Christian. Perhaps it is the person expecting that it is her right for her job to be fun and fulfilling, but when the experience of the job doesn't measure up, there is no willingness to stick at the role God has called her to do. Perhaps it is the person expecting healing, yet experiencing no improvement in her symptoms. As a result, she heads to some new ministry that declares that if you have enough faith then you will be guaranteed healing. Perhaps it is the person who expects that he will have a decent-sized house, but his experience is a cosy, adequate flat, and so he ends up with pangs of envy about his next-door neighbour's residence.

How can our christianity be marked by 100% satisfaction, even when our experiences don't meet our expectations? The answer is very simple. We don't go wider in search of new things, but rather we go deeper into what we already have.

The question is: how can our Christianity be marked by 100% satisfaction, even when our experiences don't meet our expectations? The answer is very simple. We don't go wider in search of new things, but rather we go deeper into what we already have.

Victor Hugo wrote that 'the greatest happiness of life is the conviction that we are loved'.[2] When we know we are loved, then we are content and satisfied, no matter what. It is in the context of struggles and sufferings that Paul writes about two ways that, as Christians, we know we are loved by God. The first is that 'God has poured out his love into our hearts by the Holy Spirit, whom he has given us' (Romans 5:5 NIV 1984).

The second is that 'God demonstrates his own love for us in this: while we were still sinners, Christ died for us' (Romans 5:8).

The two means of knowing God's love are through the Holy Spirit and the cross of Christ. To experience 100% satisfaction, even when there are struggles, we need to go deeper into the cross of Christ, and deeper into the Spirit of God.

1. Go deeper with the cross of Christ

a) The supremacy of love
If we want to understand the majesty and supremacy of love, we look to the cross. The cross is God's ultimate demonstration of love. In fact 'demonstrate' is too weak a word. A better translation would be 'prove'. Romans 5:8 literally says that God gives *proof* of his love for us in Christ dying for us while we were still sinners. Furthermore, the essence of love is giving, and we see in the cross of Christ the ultimate gift of the Son of God given up to death.

It is undoubtedly true that 'God so loved the world that he gave his one and only Son' (John 3:16), yet the love of God was not just for the world in general. It is also profoundly personal. In Galatians 2:20, Paul writes that 'the Son of God . . . loved me and gave himself for me'. However much you think your life is worth, Jesus loves you so much that he gave himself for you. The cross shows us how deeply personal and deeply powerful Jesus' love is for us.

In an African village, one night there was a fire. A family died in their house except for one little baby boy, saved by an unidentified figure who rushed into the inferno of flames and rescued him. Shortly afterwards the village leaders gathered to decide who should have the privilege of adopting the boy. One person put himself forward and said he was the richest in the village, so he should do it. Somebody else said that he was the most powerful, so he should do it. Another declared he was the youngest and had the energy to cope with looking after the boy. Finally, one very insignificant man stepped forward and said, 'I have a superior claim to all of you to adopt this child.'

'Why?' said the others. 'What claim have you got?'

The man slowly raised his hands for them to see. They were horribly scarred and burned.[3]

We too have a Saviour with scars. This Saviour stretches out those scarred hands and says, in effect, to each one of us, 'I have a claim on your life. I died for you. I love you.' Our dissatisfaction with God and our lot in life evaporates in the face of such love.

b) The seriousness of sin
Amazingly, understanding the scale of our sin has the same impact on us as understanding the scale of God's love – we become less dissatisfied with our circumstances.

John Owen, the famous Puritan preacher, challenged his readers to 'look on him whom you have pierced and let it trouble you'.[4] Going deeper into the cross of Christ should trouble us as we come face to face with the seriousness of our sin. For example, in the space of five verses (Romans 5:6–10),

Paul describes us all as 'powerless', 'ungodly', 'sinners' and 'God's enemies'. The result of this is that we rightly face God's wrath (5:9).

The reality is that there is such a thing as godly dissatis-faction. It is right to be dissatisfied with sin in my life. It is right to be dissatisfied with sin in the world – and to want to work against injustice and poverty. That is a godly dissatisfaction.

Yet, it is when we are most dissatisfied about sin that we find ourselves most satisfied about our circumstances. When we are focused on what really matters, it is less of an issue whether we're in plenty or in want, financially, physic-ally or emotionally. What really matters is that Christ died for us (Romans 5:6, 8). Jesus bore the penalty for sin in our place.

c) The celebration of grace

We'll never know contentment as Christians if we boast in what we do in our Christian lives, because we could always do better. We'll never be content if we boast in what we've achieved, because we could always achieve more. We'll never be content if we boast in what we've experienced, because there will always be someone else who has had a more exciting spiritual experience than us.

But when we boast in and celebrate God's grace made available to us because of Christ's death for us, then we can know contentment and satisfaction, whatever the circum-stances. The cross humbles us. Our spiritual connection to God can't be through anything we've done, or through anything we've achieved, or even through anything we've experienced. The cross of Christ is the only grounds for authentic Christian spirituality. It is because of the cross that 'we have gained access by faith into this grace in which we now stand' (Romans 5:2).

There is no room for boasting as a Christian about our own achievements (Romans 3:27). Neither is there room for boasting that God is our exclusive possession as though we were somehow superior to others who aren't trusting in Christ (Romans 2:17). Rather, the only legitimate boasting is in what God has done for us through Christ's death. It has enabled us to share in the future glory of heaven (Romans 5:2), and it has even enabled us to see the positive aspect of times of suffering and struggle (5:3). Above all, the cross has reconciled us to God (5:11).

2. Go deeper with the Holy Spirit

As we go deeper into the Holy Spirit, we realize he is not necessarily there just to sort out our problems. Primarily he is more interested in our holiness than our health or our happiness. That's why he's not called the Healthy Spirit or the Happy Spirit, but the Holy Spirit. It is true that the Spirit brings freedom, power, intimacy, expectancy and honesty, but he does so *in the context of suffering and struggle*. In the midst of a chapter with a focus on the Holy Spirit, Paul speaks of 'shar[ing] in Christ's sufferings', 'our present sufferings' and how 'we ourselves, who have the firstfruits of the Spirit, groan inwardly' (Romans 8:17, 18, 23). As we go deeper into the Holy Spirit, we are reminded that he is in operation, not primarily to remove us from the struggle and suffering, but to empower us in the midst of it all. He is still the same Holy Spirit, but in the times when our experiences have not measured up to our expectations, we can remain satisfied and content in God, rather than looking wider in a desire to improve our circumstances. The Holy Spirit brings us peace, whatever the situation.

I've always been a bit of a worrier. In fact, when I was about seven years old, my mum was talking to John, the son of our local vicar. He was about a year older than me, and was at the school that I was about to start attending.

Mum said to him, 'John, could you look after Jago when he starts at your school? Because he's a bit of a worrier.'

To which John replied, good vicar's kid that he was, 'That's OK. King David was a mighty warrior.'

And that battle has always raged within me. I long to be a mighty warrior full of peace and satisfaction, rather than a mighty worrier lacking contentment and internal peace. Paul speaks of how 'the mind controlled by the Spirit is life and peace' (Romans 8:6 NIV 1984), but very often I find it difficult to know that peace in the midst of my circumstances.

It sounds too simple to be true, but the key to knowing internal peace and satisfaction is to trust God. When our son Boaz was four, he was learning to ride his bike without stabilizers. To begin with, Boaz was rather nervous about my letting go of the bike. He lacked internal peace. However, we then came up with the solution: he would wear a small backpack with a looped handle on top (a bicycle life-jacket in effect); I would run alongside him, holding very loosely on to the handle, just in case he fell over. As soon as we did this, Boaz was suddenly a confident cycling expert – learning to cycle with great gusto and great speed. Now, he charges along far too fast for his father's liking, and it is I who have no internal peace at all as he careers among the trees on Wandsworth Common.

It is very similar with us and God. If we are feeling distant and detached from him, then it is no surprise that we lack internal peace. But if we trust him, if we know that he is, as it were, holding us by the backpack handle, then we are freed to step out and live for him and take risks for him with a great deal of peace and contentment. I love the prayer Paul prays in Romans 15:13: 'May the God of hope fill you with all joy and peace as you trust in him, so that you may overflow with hope by the power of the Holy Spirit.' God's role is to fill us with peace by the power of the Spirit. Our role is to trust him.

It is worth reflecting on where you lack internal peace at the moment. Perhaps life is stressful and your future feels very uncertain. The solution is to trust that God is great – to trust that the task ahead of you is not as great as the power of the Spirit within you.

Perhaps it's a lack of peace because of a nagging guilt for something you're doing wrong at the moment. Perhaps you are going out with someone and being too physically intimate. Then the solution is not just to say, 'Holy Spirit, please give me peace and satisfaction in this situation.' Rather, you need to trust that God is good, and by conducting your relationship in a Christ-honouring way, accept that God's ways and his standards for doing relationships are best for you.

Perhaps it's a traumatic situation you're in. Even in the obvious pain, the sorrow and the heartache, the solution is to trust that God is gracious and that he cares for you and knows your pains and can supply all your needs in the midst of the suffering, even if he doesn't take you out of the situation.

There may still be times of struggle and pain, just as Boaz had with his bike riding, but just as he could trust that his father was holding him and would care for him, how much more can we trust our great, good and gracious God to hold us and give us all that we need?[5]

For fourteen years, I met with three friends to pray and be accountable with each other. A few years ago, one of them went through a particularly bad time. His pregnant wife was diagnosed with a type of cancer – lymphoma. She had chemotherapy with the hope that she would recover and that the baby would be fine, but then, just a week before the baby was due to arrive, the little boy died in her womb and was stillborn. His wife is now well, but it was an awful time.

Yet it was also amazing to see my friends trusting God even in the most seemingly horrendous of times. They felt agony and confusion and gut-wrenching anguish. But they kept their trust in God. This is a couple of lines from an email they sent five days after their son's death: 'In the midst of our grief and disbelief we are confident that our God is the same loving, generous and powerful Father he has always been. Right at the heart of our pain we have found a peace that does pass all human understanding.'

The God of hope filled them with internal peace as they trusted in him. He filled them, and he can fill us too.

The foundation for satisfaction: eternal peace and eternal love

There is a right dissatisfaction with this world. The world is not as it should be. God forbid that we become apathetic. When we see an old man homeless in the depths of winter, with only a bottle of extra-strong cider to keep him company, we should declare this is not as things should be. When we see television images of a child dying of starvation, we should not just 'pass by on the other side' (see Luke 10:31–32). It is right that our discontent should be real, and should spur us to action. And yet, when we face struggles or hardships or sufferings in our own lives, these need not cause us to become dissatisfied with God, to start detaching the red Lego block.

We can only know internal peace and satisfaction and contentment in hard circumstances, when we recognize first and foremost the eternal peace with God that we possess in Christ. Paul writes, 'Since we have been justified through faith, we have peace with God through our Lord Jesus Christ' (Romans 5:1). If we know peace with God, the reality is that whatever situation we find ourselves in, we can rest our head on the pillow at the end of each day and be satisfied, because ultimately everything is OK.

This peace with God, which was made available through the cross, is eternal. Very near the end of the whole letter, Paul reminds the Romans that there will come a time when our God of peace will bring about total peace for eternity. He declares that 'the God of peace will soon crush Satan under your feet' (Romans 16:20). He's pointing forwards to the time in the future when God will wrap up this world as we know it, and there will be a new heaven and a new earth with no more death or mourning or crying or pain or suffering or war.

During World War 2, there was a problem in Britain's coalmines. Knowing the nation's need, and wanting to participate more directly in the effort to defend the UK, many of the miners were inclined to leave their difficult, thankless jobs in the pits and join the army instead. They wanted to be a part of something bigger, more glorious and more meaningful.

However, this was a problem because the war effort desperately needed the coal that these miners brought up out of the ground every day. So one day Winston Churchill spoke to the miners, and he surprised them with what he said. He told them that their dirty, grimy jobs were just as important in the war effort as anyone else's. He asked them to picture in their minds the grand parade that would take place when the work of the war had come to its conclusion and victory finally came. Their children and grandchildren would be watching to catch a glimpse of the heroes who had secured their freedom.

First in the parade, Churchill said, would come the sailors of the Navy, the same kind of people as the heroes of Trafalgar and the defeat of the Armada generations before. Next in the parade, he went on, would come the pilots of the Royal Air Force, the few to whom so many owed so much, because their skills and bravery, more than any others, had defended England's skies from the dreaded German Luftwaffe. Then the heroes of the Army would march by, those who had stood tall at Dunkirk and taken the battle to the enemy.

But at the end of the parade, said Churchill, would come a long line of sweat-stained, soot-streaked men in miners' caps. Someone seeing them would cry from the crowd, 'Where were you during the critical days of the struggle?' From ten thousand throats would come the proud answer: 'We were deep in the earth with our faces to the coal.'

We are told there were tears visible on the soot-laden and weathered faces of those miners as they listened to the prime minister that day. They returned to the pits with their shoulders straighter and their heads held higher, ready for the task in hand.

We're often in the same kind of situation as those miners. We get so focused on the pain or dirt or difficulty or drudgery of our lives that we lack internal peace and satisfaction. We feel like we're stuck in the pit of thankless jobs or endless responsibilities. But what brings internal peace and satisfaction, in the midst of struggle and conflict and challenge, is clarity on the eternal peace of the future, made possible at the cross.

One day there will be a victory parade that all Christians will be part of, an event far more glorious and permanent than the one Churchill described. It will be a victory parade celebrating eternal peace. But it will also be a celebration of eternal love.

Of course, it is true that when our experiences don't meet our expectations, we are tempted to think that God has deserted us and stopped loving us. It is a question I find that I get asked again and again in pastoral situations. When tough times come, we doubt whether God still loves us. Paul asks this very question: 'Who shall separate us from the love of Christ? Shall trouble or hardship or persecution or famine or nakedness or danger or sword?', but his reply is that the Christian cannot be separated from the love of Christ because 'in all these things we are more than conquerors through him who loved us' (Romans 8:35, 37). The conquering victors – all Christians – will celebrate eternal love as well as eternal peace.

However, notice that Paul writes 'through him who loved us'. Of course Christ loves us in the present and he will love us in the future, but the key thing that Paul is emphasizing is that Christ loved us in the past. He has shown his love, in the past, through his death on the cross. The God of all the universe is totally committed to us for eternity – and that is guaranteed because of the cross. That is why we can be convinced that 'neither death nor life, neither angels nor demons, neither the present nor the future, nor any powers, neither height nor depth, nor anything else in all creation, will be able to separate us from the love of God that is in Christ Jesus our Lord' (Romans 8:38–39). Just as the peace with God which was made available through the cross is an eternal peace, so too the love of God which was displayed at the cross is an eternal love.

Suffering can't be avoided. We will face struggles. Overall, this life is marked more by groaning than glory. But Jesus hasn't deserted us, even when it feels like he has. Even when we are totally dissatisfied *with* the situation we are in, we can still know satisfaction *in* the midst of it. Eternal love and eternal peace are ours in Christ, enabled because of the cross, and experienced because of the Spirit.

100% activation

The last couple of years have been a challenge for me. Aged twenty-five, my husband left me. I then had two years of chronic insomnia, constant headaches and migraines, and a loss of belief in a good God. During this time I got meningitis. I wrote the following journal entry while I was in hospital battling the meningitis, struggling to make sense of all that had happened despite endless prayer and faith. At this time I felt like I had to stop running and fighting in the dark and finally admit surrender, and try to reconnect with God.

Stop and question: 'Why, God?'
Eyes sinking into a puffed-up face
My chest rumbling with germs
Head pounding, heavy on a tight neck
Light and noise grating, scratching tender nerves

Beep, beep, beep . . . endless sounds the drip that
        has held me hostage in this bed
Testing me with Chinese torture
Alone in this room
Taken out of the world and its noise for a while
Forced to feel and face up to my new reality

I yearn to know you again, God
To have you close and hear your voice.
Three years' worth of prayers, abandoned
You turned your face from my fasting
And your touch from my heart

I can't understand why you watched my heart breaking
Yet remained silent to my cries,
Why you watched as my world turned upside down
And didn't intervene

People let me down
But you are meant to hold me up
So many sufferings in this broken world
And where are you?

I watch them jump and dance, singing praises
But my soul feels despondent and disappointed,
      disillusioned by it all

I pray for you to meet me, but you don't show
I ask for things and the opposite happens

You don't seem to hear my prayers
But I want to talk with you

You keep your voice from me
But I want to hear

I don't understand your ways
I am trying to hope
I ask such simple things from you
They go unanswered into an empty night

I ask for your angels to comfort me
But toss and turn into the dawn

How long must I be in Gethsemane?
For how long will you keep yourself from me?

Sometimes I can see that
Maybe you have kept me sane
Perhaps angels have held me in the dark
Have you been there all along?
Mysterious one, who can know your ways?
(Clare Cardy, therapist)

100% adoration

Heavenly Father, where my experience doesn't match
     my expectations,
     please help me to know that you still love me and
          are there for me.
May I truly be convinced that neither death nor life,
     neither angels nor demons,
     neither the present nor the future,
     nor any powers,
     neither height nor depth,
     nor anything else in all creation,
will be able to separate me from your love that is in
          Christ Jesus my Lord.
Amen.

6. Christianity is 100% satisfaction

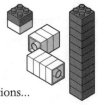

When our experience does not meet our expectations...

1) Go deeper with the cross of Christ

- a) The supremacy of love
- b) The seriousness of sin
- c) The celebration of grace

2) Go deeper with the Holy Spirit

The foundation for satisfaction: **eternal peace** *and* **eternal love**

100% application

1. Where are your experiences not meeting your expectations?
2. Where are you dissatisfied with life? Why is it making you dissatisfied? How can you know satisfaction in your life?
3. 'God's role is to fill us with peace by the power of the Spirit. Our role is to trust him.' Why do you find it difficult to believe that God is good, great and gracious?
4. How do you know that Jesus has not deserted you?

Read Romans 5, 8.

PART 3: 100% LIFE

In 2004, Ruth Kelly was made Secretary of State for Education in the UK, and much was written about her Christian beliefs and whether they were compatible with being in charge of education for the country. She was interviewed by the *Daily Mirror*, and this is what she said: 'I have a private spiritual life and I have a faith. I have a private spiritual life, and I don't think it is relevant to my job.'[1] Matthew Parris, *The Times* newspaper columnist and former MP who is quick to declare that he is not a Christian, responded to Ruth Kelly's comment the next day. He stated: 'That is wholly inconsistent . . . with Christ's teaching. Of course one's faith, and the moral code anchored in it, is relevant to one's job. It is impossible to read the Gospels in any other way.'[2]

Matthew Parris, I believe, is right. So many people try to compartmentalize their lives, but that is not the call of the gospel. Who we are and how we act at work, for example, should be the same as who we are and how we act at church. Our Christian faith should have an impact on us in 100% of life. Making a divide between what is sacred and important to God, and what is secular and unimportant to God, has been one of the most common mistakes in the church throughout the ages.

There has always been a tendency to compartmentalize and divide what should be held together. A biblical example is the Corinthian church. It seems that the Corinthians had absorbed too much of the culture in which they lived, including the philosophy of Plato, who saw the body as inferior to the soul. With classic Greek humour, Plato used a play on words to describe the body (*soma*) as a tomb (*sema*) which acted as a prison for the soul. The Corinthian Christians therefore began to think that it did not matter what took place in their bodies, because the body was only a temporary construct while the soul was just waiting to escape the prison of the body. Again, they came to believe that the possession of spiritual gifts such as speaking in tongues, rather than one's behaviour day to day in the body, was a true sign of spirituality. They therefore related to their bodies by either ruthlessly satisfying their bodily needs (hedonism; for example, 1 Corinthians 6:12–20), or ruthlessly denying their bodily needs (asceticism; for example, 1 Corinthians 7:1–4). Paul's whole teaching in 1 Corinthians aims to raise the importance of the body, in the present and in the future. He shows how, in the future, God will glorify the believer's body (1 Corinthians 15:43), but in the present, the believer's body is to glorify God (1 Corinthians 6:20; 10:31). His point is that we should never see what we do with our bodies as unimportant to God – Christianity is about 100% of life.

Even some of the spiritual giants of the faith have been in danger of compartmentalizing and creating a sacred–secular divide. Augustine used to view the 'active' life (everyday activity in the world) as inferior to the 'contemplative' life of religious activity.[3] Antony, the most famous of the fourth-century desert fathers, often refused to speak to people, and on one occasion he said that 'just as fish taken out of the water soon die on dry land, so too, monks who stay with people from the world are soon weakened by human conversations'.[4] Benedict in the fifth and sixth centuries ensured that his monasteries had everything that was needed within them 'so that the monks do not need to wander about outside, for this is not at all good for their souls'.[5] All of them implied that God was not interested in some parts of life, and that a division should be made between the sacred and the secular.

Today we are often no better. John Stott often used to say that Jesus Christ is either Lord of all, or he is not Lord at all. We can be guilty in many different ways of not letting Jesus be Lord in all areas of life. Just as Augustine, Antony and Benedict differentiated between different spheres of life, so we start believing that what takes place under the physical roof of the church is more significant and of more importance to God than what goes on away from the church building.

Mark Greene, writing to church leaders, comments that 'there is a danger that we will view church members exclusively in terms of how they can contribute to the church in the neighbourhood, rather than how they might contribute to the growth of the kingdom of Christ, wherever he has placed them'.[6] Yet, if all the world lies under the lordship of Christ, then there can be no segment of life divorced from his influence and no place where the red Lego block of the gospel is not relevant.

Similarly, just as the Corinthians held up a division between the body and soul, so we can be guilty of believing that a vertical relationship with God can be divorced from a horizontal relationship with the world, under the mistaken belief that the vertical is 'spiritual' and the horizontal is merely about 'matter'. The reality is that how we live in this world is vitally important.

One hundred per cent Christianity must have an impact in 100% of life – for all people, in all places, at all times.

7. CHRISTIANITY IS 100% INCLUSIVE

(Romans 9 – 11)

> As the Scripture says, 'Anyone who trusts in him will never
> be put to shame.' For there is no difference between Jew
> and Gentile – the same Lord is Lord of all and richly blesses
> all who call on him, for, 'Everyone who calls on the name
> of the Lord will be saved.'
>
> (Romans 10:11–13)

The words 'inclusive' and 'exclusive' carry so much weight and
baggage today. In some contexts they're really positive words,
but in other contexts they are deeply negative. Take the word
'exclusive'. Lots of sporting institutions have over recent years
made their membership open to women as well as men,
because they were accused of being exclusive – out of touch,
offensive – by only opening their doors to men. Exclusivity in
that context is seen to be a bad thing.

But then take *Hello!* magazine. Regularly it will have the
word 'Exclusive' emblazoned on its front cover because its
editors have gained exclusive rights to take photographs at
some B-list celebrity wedding. Being 'exclusive' there is seen
to be a good thing – that's why they splash the word across
the pages. No-one is going around offended that *Hello!*
magazine is exclusively providing us with pictures of the

happy couple dancing and cutting their cake and snuggling on a deluxe sofa.

However, a problem would rear its head if the publishers of *Hello!* decided to be exclusive over who was allowed to buy their magazine. If you were only allowed to buy this magazine if you were a woman, or if you lived in Grimsby, or if you were left-handed, then that would be exclusive in a bad way. As long as you're prepared to give *Hello!* the cost of the magazine, then there should be total inclusivity over who can see the exclusive wedding pictures it provides.

Now transfer this discussion to the arena of Christianity. With great regularity, I find myself having conversations with people who state that the Christian claim that the only way to God is through faith in Jesus seems arrogant, unfair and exclusive. Christianity is seen to be exclusive in the bad sense of the word.

I wonder what you think. Is Christianity inclusive or exclusive? And in a good way or a bad way? Paul's answer to the Christians in Rome is surprising.

1. Christianity is exclusive (Romans 9:1 – 10:4)

Again and again, we are reminded by Paul that no-one deserves to be right with God. God is holy and we are not. It is only by his mercy that any of us are saved and enter into a right relationship with him (Romans 9:16). If there were going to be any exceptions to this, it would be the devout Israelite. The people of Israel were God's chosen people. Paul loved the Jewish people – after all, he was a Jew himself. He tells the Roman Christians that his 'heart's desire and prayer to God for the Israelites is that they may be saved' (Romans 10:1). There's no doubt that many of these Israelites were devout and moral and sincere: 'they are zealous for God' (Romans 10:2).

Yet being a devout Jew doesn't make someone right with God, for 'since they did not know the righteousness that comes from God and sought to establish their own, they did not submit to God's righteousness' (Romans 10:3). The exclusive claim of the apostle Paul is that even a zealous, sincere, devout Jewish person cannot get right with God unless he or she trusts in Jesus.

This may sound an arrogant claim, but actually it is just what Jesus himself said. Possibly Jesus' most famous encounter ever was with Nicodemus, one of Israel's head teachers.[1] He was a member of the Jewish ruling council. If ever there was someone who was going to be accepted by God on religious or moral grounds, it was Nicodemus. Yet Jesus' very first words to Nicodemus were, 'Very truly I tell you, no one can see the kingdom of God unless they are born again' (John 3:3). Even in conversation with a man like Nicodemus, Jesus says that someone can't be in a right relationship with God unless they are completely remade. Indeed, as the discussion with Nicodemus continues, Jesus clarifies what he means. He speaks of needing to be 'born of the Spirit' (John 3:8) and of how everyone who believes in him has eternal life (John 3:16).

The testimony of Jesus and Paul is that every one of us needs to trust in Jesus as our Lord to be saved. Just as *Hello!* magazine is the exclusive place for certain pictures from celebrity weddings, so Christianity is the exclusive place to get right with God. Belief in Jesus as Lord is the only way to be saved. Christianity is exclusive. Everyone needs to trust in Jesus as their Lord.

2. Christianity is inclusive (Romans 10:5–13)

However, just when you thought you were clear about the exclusivity of Christianity, Paul seems to change tack and starts showing how inclusive Christianity is. He is at pains to demonstrate that the offer of right standing with God through faith in Jesus is open to all. It is inclusive. We don't have to ascend into heaven or descend into the deep to find Jesus (Romans 10:6–7). Jesus is easily accessible to us all. He has come down, died for us and risen again. We don't have to go anywhere or do anything.

It doesn't matter who we are. 'If you confess with your mouth, "Jesus is Lord," and believe in your heart that God raised him from the dead, you will be saved' (Romans 10:9 NIV 1984). Inward belief is combined with outward confession. We simply trust – personally and publicly – in Jesus. Furthermore, everyone is included in this offer. Notice the way Paul emphasizes the inclusivity of the offer. He says,

> As the Scripture says, '*Anyone* who trusts in him will never be put to shame.' For there is no difference between Jew and Gentile – the same Lord is Lord of *all* and richly blesses *all* who call on him, for, '*Everyone* who calls on the name of the Lord will be saved.'
> (Romans 10:11–13 NIV 1984, my italics).

As a young Christian, I went out to Borneo to teach English in a Bible college. I was only eighteen at the time, had been a Christian for less than a year, and had lived a fairly sheltered and privileged life. The Bible college was in the foothills of Mount Kinabalu, and the men and women were as different in background from me as was possible. Our skin colour was different. Our level of education was different. Our level of wealth was different. My friend and I expected them to have witnessed lots of death through tribal in-fighting. They expected us to have witnessed lots of death through the gun crime that they saw on the one television in the college. Yet, despite all that might have divided us, I learned more from those people about my relationship with Jesus Christ than I have over any other three-month period. They showed me that Jesus is easily and equally accessible.

> *The fact that Christianity is exclusive means that everyone needs to trust in Jesus as their Lord, and the fact that it is inclusive means that anyone can trust in Jesus as their Lord.*

It can sometimes seem as though you have to be a particular type of person to be a Christian: 'Sorry. You can't be a Christian. You're not good enough.' 'Sorry. You can't be a Christian. You live in the wrong country.' 'Sorry. You can't be a Christian. You've got a tongue stud and you don't like organ music.' But this is not true. The offer of being in right relationship with God through accepting Jesus as one's Lord is 100% inclusive. Anyone can trust in Jesus as their Lord.

We need beautiful feet (Romans 10:14–15)

The fact that Christianity is exclusive means that *everyone* needs to trust in Jesus as their Lord, and the fact that it is inclusive means that *anyone* can trust in Jesus as their Lord.

For the Christian, the application is clear: we need to speak of Jesus with all people:

How, then, can they call on the one they have not believed in?
And how can they believe in the one of whom they have not
heard? And how can they hear without someone preaching
to them? And how can anyone preach unless they are sent?
As it is written: 'How beautiful are the feet of those who
bring good news!'
(Romans 10:14–15)

We need to be people with beautiful feet. The logic is com-
pelling. Everyone who calls on the name of the Lord will be
saved (v. 13). People can't call on the Lord if they haven't
believed the evidence for Christ (v. 14a). People can't believe
the evidence for Christ if they have not heard it presented to
them (v. 14b). We won't present Christ to others with our
words unless we feel we have been sent and commissioned
(v. 15a). Yet we have been commissioned and sent to speak the
good news about Christ (v. 15b).

You're bound to have heard the oft-stated misquotation
from St Francis of Assisi: 'Preach the gospel at all times; if
necessary use words.' This is generally taken by people to
mean that if we live an amazingly moral and kind life, then
we don't really need to use words to witness to Jesus. However,
I'd like to challenge that assumption.

Let your imagination run wild with me for a moment . . .
You are the kindest, most impressive person in your workplace (you may have to imagine very hard). In fact, you are so
magnificent that your colleagues hate it when you go on holiday
because they love your friendship so much. Without you, your
colleagues can't cope. They often come to you for advice
whenever there's a problem, professional or personal. You've
always got time for them and you never utter a cross word to
anyone. They respect you for the person you are and the job
you do. Very simply, you've become a legend in your workplace.

However, the million-dollar question is this: despite being the most popular person in your workplace, loved by everyone, respected by all, are you bringing others to delight in the glory of God? The answer is: not necessarily. Because, if no-one knows you're a Christian, then your incredible lifestyle glorifies you.[2]

In my experience, most of us who are Christians recognize that it is important for people to know that we are Christians. There are some who live a double life for a while – hiding their connection to Christ at work, or at the sports club, or during Freshers' Week. But it is not desirable or viable.

However, for those of us who are open about the fact that we are a Christian, I don't think we can rest in a self-satisfied glow of holiness.

Let's return to our fantasy world. We are the greatest, most lovable person in our workplace, and yet the truth is that it still doesn't necessarily bring others to recognize the glory of God even if people know that we're a Christian. If all our colleagues know is that we live an awesome lifestyle, and that we are a Christian, but that's all they know, then they will probably conclude that the Christian gospel instructs us to be good and moral and kind in order to earn our way to heaven. And of course that is the opposite of the Christian gospel. They will get completely the wrong idea about Christianity, and God will not be glorified.

To bring others to glorify God, we need to help them get to know the good news about the gospel. This isn't easy. I'm not saying that you should go and stand on a soapbox and start preaching to all your colleagues, friends, teammates, and so on. But I am saying that this is generally the biggest challenge of evangelism – how to move from telling people you're a Christian and saying that you go to church, to actually speaking the good news about Jesus. It's my biggest challenge.

But we must meet this challenge, because 'faith comes from hearing the message, and the message is heard through the word of Christ' (Romans 10:17 NIV 1984).

Of course, the way we live and work matters intensely. Of course, our attitudes and motives and the desires of our hearts are crucial. In our workplaces, the work we do will either promote the good news of Christ or bring the good news into disrepute. In life, how I act will either make the gospel more attractive to people I come into contact with, or give them extra reason to have nothing more to do with Jesus. Yet the way in which we live and work will not in itself communicate the good news about Christ. Our life needs to be combined with our lips. Or, in the language of Romans, we need to be people with beautiful feet – whoever we are, and wherever we are.

God has beautiful hands (Romans 10:16–21)

I'll be honest. There are times when I'm not very keen to tell others about Jesus. I'm afraid or embarrassed or fearful or just not very passionate. Often that desire to tell others seems to decrease the longer you have been a Christian. People are really enthusiastic to tell others about Jesus when they first become a Christian, but then the enthusiasm cools.

Generally, the main reason for this cooling is because we find that not everyone responds positively to the good news of Jesus. We've told people in the past, but they reject what they hear. We tell others, and they reject it too, and we so get downbeat and disheartened, and don't think it's worth telling people any more. If I think back to my time at university, or as a management consultant, in both cases the number of conversations about Jesus I had in the three years of university or the five years of being a management consultant decreased over that period. This was because people generally rejected the gospel when we chatted in the early months, and so I was reticent to continue speaking of Jesus as time wore on. I did not want to experience more rejection.

This is what happened as the early Christians spoke of Jesus with many of the Jewish people in Paul's time. They heard the message about Christ (Romans 10:17), but not all of them accepted it (Romans 10:16). The encouragement for us is that we are not the only ones who feel rejected. God feels rejected too.

As we speak of him, he is standing there too – with his hands out, offering people a relationship with him. He has beautiful hands, but some reject what he is offering. God says, 'All day long I have held out my hands to a disobedient and obstinate people' (Romans 10:21).

Think of a sea anemone fastened to the side of a rock pool when the tide comes up.[3] It's all closed up like a little cherry, until the tide reaches it and the rock pool is flooded with water, and then suddenly out come these long wavy tentacles that sway in the water. There is nothing whatsoever that the little anemone can do to bring the tide in or to stop it coming in. All it can do is choose to open up its tentacles as the water floods over it. Or it could choose to stay closed.

Similarly, we can do nothing whatsoever to bring the tide of God's grace into our lives, nor can we stop it. We are not in control of it. The wonderful truth is that it has gone out into all the earth – not as a tide of water, but as a voice (Romans 10:18). Yet tragically, some stay closed to that message, not opening up their tentacles to the grace of God, and not reaching out to God's beautiful outstretched hands – hands that have been pierced for us to pay for our sin.

Blood, rash and tears

I don't claim to be an Old Testament prophet. I've never had an actual vision of the Lord seated on his throne like Isaiah (Isaiah 6). I have never taken it upon myself to start smearing blood around the place to bring purity like Ezekiel (Ezekiel 43). However, when I was preaching on Romans 10 at Holy Trinity Clapham, something rather strange did happen. In the few days leading up to the sermon, I developed a rash on my hands and feet. I've never had it before or since. I felt as though it were a visual picture of what we needed to pray for as a church family. My hunch was that there were people in the church who saw God's hands as rashy. They didn't want to stretch out and hold God's hands, because they saw the good news of the gospel as bad news. I also felt that there were many in the church who had spiritually rashy feet, because we had not been proclaiming the good news of Jesus as we should have been. It was a powerful time for many as we prayed about our 'rashy' hands and feet. I was one who prayed to have beautiful feet again as I allowed the Spirit to work in me to give me a greater passion and boldness to speak of Jesus with those who don't yet know him.

That night, as I preached on Romans 10, I finished the sermon by referring to the time when I cried while giving a best man's speech at a wedding. Maybe the bride might shed a few tears on her wedding day, but generally not the best man. I tried to focus on entertainment and humour, dishing the dirt on the groom. But then, rather embarrassingly, during the best man's speech, I started blubbing like a baby.

This is the reason for the waterworks. In my speech, I said these words: 'The second reason I am indebted to Andy [my friend, the bridegroom] is that he introduced me to Jesus Christ. When Andy was sixteen he became a Christian, asking

Jesus to be his Lord and Saviour. About a year later, Andy asked me if I wanted to come with him on a three-day conference for people in the sixth form at school to investigate Christianity. I really didn't want to go – but I did. And it was there that I realized that the Christian message is true and that I couldn't keep on running away from God . . . And I am so grateful to God that he used Andy to bring me to a point where I accepted Jesus as my Lord.'

I said that last line choked up with tears. I cried because of Andy's 'beautiful feet'. As Paul says, 'How beautiful are the feet of those who bring good news!' (Romans 10:15). My prayer is that you, reading this book, and me writing it, may have feet that are beautiful enough to bring tears of joy to others as we, however falteringly and feebly, speak the good news of Jesus, the one who holds out his beautiful but pierced hands towards us all. It is the most exclusive of all offers – the one and only way to get right with God. And it is an offer that is totally inclusive, open to all.

100% activation

'When you hear God's call you will not mistake it.' Those were the words my amazing dear mother spoke to me when I was arrested for the first time. They were often repeated by her whenever disaster struck in my life, usually as a result of the choices I made. She has been an immeasurable blessing in my life. Both she and my father prayed for me for over twenty years that I might become a Christian and actually come to know God.

I was thirty-six when I became a Christian. I was brought up as a Catholic and went to church every week out of habit and family tradition rather than anything else. I didn't ever contemplate that it was even possible to have an intimate relationship with God the

Father through Jesus and the Holy Spirit. With the benefit of hindsight and personal experience, I can now say undoubtedly that I wasn't a Christian for the first thirty-six years of my life.

In truth I was lost, broken and desperate throughout the first period of my life up until I became a Christian. I felt excluded in all areas of my life. I was blessed to be naturally academic and good at sport while growing up. I came from a good, stable family and things were relatively easy for me until, aged twelve, I was bullied. The colour of my skin became a focus for bullying, and I quickly went into and remained in a place of personal pain. To protect myself, and to try to attain acceptance and love, I eventually lashed out. I put up a mask of protection and pretended to be something I wasn't. The kind, gentle boy that my parents knew quickly disappeared. He was replaced by a difficult, disruptive and unhappy person who began playing truant and running with local gangs.

Before long, the A grades turned to D grades, a life of crime escalated, and by age twenty-one I had become involved with the criminal underworld, a football hooligan known across London, leading a life focused on drink, drugs, the guest list of private parties and the best nightclubs and restaurants, the best designer clothes, and everything that came with a celebrity lifestyle.

I was worshipped and put on a pedestal. It was an adrenalin-fuelled lifestyle and I was a rascal of the highest order. I never considered myself to be a nasty or bad person. Despite everything, I always felt I had a good heart and was desperate to take the mask down and show people who I really was. I couldn't do it, out of sheer fear and pain.

I had, quite literally, hundreds of people and friends around me throughout that period. I mixed with famous people and villains alike and had relationships with beautiful women. Of course, none of it satisfied me spiritually. At the heart of it was a longing for acceptance and love. I didn't feel good enough for anyone, let alone God. I had no comprehension of God's love and forgiveness. The shy and gentle man behind the mask did not emerge and, in fact, could not until I was set free by God's grace.

It wasn't until 5 February 1995 that things began to change for me. Disaster struck. I was in a horrific car crash in Sussex where tragically my friend died and there was another fatality. My friend died on top of me, and I witnessed a terrible scene and severe injuries. I was very lucky to survive, and went into a coma for a short period. It was at the crash site that I had an out-of-body experience and became aware of the presence of God for the first time.

As I recovered in the months that followed, the shutter came down on my former life. I was not ready to take my mask down and didn't know how to in reality. All I knew was that God existed. I wanted to turn my life around and to be a good or better person. I recovered physically and mentally over time, and went to university to study law, eventually by the grace of God qualifying as a lawyer and beginning to practise. I led a very quiet life by anyone's standards. It was what I needed after the madness of so many years. What I didn't know or understand, however, was how to access God. I still felt isolated and excluded within the legal profession. Even though I led a much better life than previously, I was still searching for real meaning and purpose. I had begun going to church again but was still very much lost and isolated, just in a different way.

It wasn't until the summer of 2003 that a close Christian friend of mine came alongside me when I was challenged again by life's ups and downs. A long-term relationship had ended, my relationship with my father had become fraught, more so than ever before, and my principal at the law firm where I worked was trying to bully me. I was very low. I asked myself, 'How can this happen to me when I lead such a good life now?' I saw a peace in my friend that defied all logic and understanding. He had been a heroin addict and an alcoholic, but had been set free from his addictions and seemed incredibly happy and grounded. He witnessed to me in a very gentle and loving way.

After a couple of months I asked him, 'What is it with you? Despite your addictions and all your troubles you seem so peaceful. Look at me – I lead such a good and simple life now compared to my past, but everything still goes wrong and I just don't get it.'

He answered, 'I think your heart is open and you are ready to listen for the first time. If you want to know the meaning of life, the only reason we are on this planet is to come into a relationship with our Maker, Jesus Christ.'

In that moment, the Holy Spirit came upon me in the most powerful way. I was convicted and converted instantly, and dropped to my knees and gave my life to God. I thanked God for saving me and loving me there and then. I knew it with all my heart, and for the first time I understood the words of my mother as I heard God's call on my life.

I have never looked back. I know that I am called to serve God in my life. We all are, however that may be. There are struggles of course that come with life, but God equips you to deal with everything. He gives us what we need, not what we want or think we need. I do find it difficult to be obedient and to trust God, but despite that and all my failings, he loves me unconditionally. It is only through my relationship with God through Jesus that I have ever felt able to take my mask down and to reveal the real man. I've met and mixed with some villains in my time, but I am no tough guy.

There is a spiritual hunger in all of us that can only be satisfied by one all-inclusive, all-loving, unconditional relationship. I know that without God's grace and forgiveness, together with a continuing relationship with God through the Holy Spirit, the changes I have made in my life would not have been possible. The difference is immeasurable. Being able to serve him in the things I now do, whether it is prison ministry, praying for others, leading an Alpha course, or simply just trying to be a good witness for God on a daily basis in my life at work and with friends and strangers alike, has given my life real purpose. Of course I often fail and fall short, but God always forgives and helps me back onto my feet every time, so I can start each day with renewed hope in Christ Jesus.

(Keith Lobo, lawyer)

100% adoration

Lord Jesus, thank you that you are the only way to the Father,
   and that everyone who calls on your name and trusts you
      as their Lord will be saved.
Thank you for your amazing love and mercy.
Please help me to be someone with beautiful feet
   by bringing the good news about you to those I come into
      contact with.
Please help me not just to tell people that I'm a Christian,
   but to actually speak about the good news with them.
Thank you that, whoever I am speaking to, the gospel is
      good news for them.
Amen.

7. Christianity is 100% inclusive

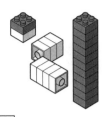

1) Christianity is **exclusive** *(9:1 – 10:4)*

> Everyone needs to trust in Jesus as their Lord

2) Christianity is **inclusive** *(10:5–13)*

> Anyone can trust in Jesus as their Lord

We need beautiful feet *(10:14–15)*
God has beautiful hands *(10:16–21)*

100% application

1. Do you agree that everyone needs to trust in Jesus as their Lord?
2. Are there ways that you act, or you have seen other people act, which might cause others to think that you have to be 'a certain type of person' to be a Christian?
3. How are your lips and your life promoting the good news of Jesus?
4. Are your feet 'rashy'? Do you sometimes believe God's hands are 'rashy'? How will you pray about this?

Read Romans 9 – 11.

8. CHRISTIANITY IS 100% INTER-RELATIONAL

(Romans 12 – 13)

> Therefore, I urge you, brothers [and sisters], in view of
> God's mercy, to offer your bodies as living sacrifices, holy
> and pleasing to God – this is your spiritual act of worship.
> Do not conform any longer to the pattern of this world,
> but be transformed by the renewing of your mind. Then
> you will be able to test and approve what God's will is –
> his good, pleasing and perfect will.
>
> (Romans 12:1–2 NIV 1984)

Harold Jelicoe Percival served as ground crew during the
Dambusters raid in World War 2. He never married, and had
no children. He died aged ninety-nine, and his funeral was at
11 am on 11 November 2013. His distant family expected only
two or three people to be there. However, the funeral director
put an advert in a newspaper appealing for people to attend.
Over 700 mourners responded to the call.

We all instinctively know that relationships are important.
We feel sorry for someone who seems isolated and alone.
Relationships are what make us tick. Loneliness is so painful.
One godly Christian woman in church emailed my wife
and me recently. 'Don't get me wrong,' she wrote. 'I'm not
desperate to find a husband; I'm just desperately lonely.

I'm not sure how long I'll be able to handle the loneliness I feel.'

We all long for good, loving relationships with others. We desire them with a passion. And yet there is a problem. For me, certainly, it is in my relationships that most of my sin is carried out. So take my marriage to Susannah. She is the person on this earth that I love the most and care for the most and put myself out for the most. Yet she is also the person on this earth that I have hurt and offended the most.

Or take church. We've all heard the old adage: if you find a perfect church, don't join it, because you will spoil it. Church is generally wonderful – apart from having to relate to some of the more difficult people who are a part of it.

In all areas of life, the biggest challenge is how we relate to other people.

Or take work. What do you complain about most connected to your work? For most of us it is some of the people we work with. They are a pain. They are obnoxious. They are useless. They are unthoughtful. They don't pay us enough.

Again and again, in all areas of life, the biggest challenge is how we relate to other people. We are inter-relational beings, and we need God to transform our relationships by the work of his Spirit.

Our 'spiritual act of worship', which Paul speaks of in Romans 12:1, is surprisingly not about our religious rituals, but about our relationships. If you or I want to assess how we are doing as worshippers of God, the first thing to examine is our relationships. And if you are anything like me, when you do that assessment, you will be crying out to God for his help so that you are no longer conformed to the pattern of this world, but transformed in how you do relationships by the renewing of your mind (Romans 12:2).

Our relationship with ourselves transformed

The first relationship to be transformed is the relationship with the person in life whom we love the most, who we think is the most wonderful, yet who is also the most difficult and most frustrating – ourselves. It is so easy for us to get too big for our boots, but Paul writes that 'by the grace given me I say to every one of you: Do not think of yourself more highly than you ought, but rather think of yourself with sober judgment, in accordance with the measure of faith God has given you' (Romans 12:3).

We all need this transformation. Recently I was complaining at length about some situation to Susannah. My wife listened patiently, and then replied with a statement that took me totally by surprise: 'What you're really saying is that you want everyone else in the world to be just like you, and if everyone else was like you, then this situation would get sorted.'

I gasped with shock at the audacity of my wife. I got cross with her, and told her that what she was saying was quite ridiculous. But as I thought about her comment during the next twenty-four hours, I realized that she had hit the proverbial nail on the head. She had challenged my ugly, self-centred, self-righteous pride to the core.

I certainly need transforming, and God transforms us to view ourselves with *humility rather than pride*. Take John Newton's words. He wrote the famous hymn 'Amazing Grace', which was born out of personal experience of the grace of God. He was the captain of a slave-trading ship.

Before he became a Christian, John Newton was a massive drinker, and he used to have sex with any of the female slaves he liked. He was full of arrogance and pride. In fact, it took years after becoming a Christian for God to change those areas of Newton's life. However, towards the end of his life, this is what he wrote:

> I am not what I ought to be – ah, how imperfect and deficient! I
> am not what I wish to be – I abhor what is evil, and I would cleave
> to what is good! I am not what I hope to be – soon, soon shall I
> put off mortality, and with mortality all sin and imperfection. Yet,
> though I am not what I ought to be, nor what I wish to be, nor
> what I hope to be, I can truly say, I am not what I once was.[1]

These are amazing words, demonstrating how Newton's mind had been transformed in his relationship to himself. No longer puffed up with pride or self-righteousness, no longer pulled down by guilt and regret and a morbid introspection, but rather making a right judgment on his status and thankful to God for all the transformation that had occurred in his life.

Our relationship with Christians transformed

Paul takes the picture of our individual bodies, which we offer to him as living sacrifices, and he goes on to use it as a picture of the church as one body with many parts: 'Just as each of us has one body with many members, and these members do not all have the same function, so in Christ we, though many, form one body, and each member belongs to all the others' (Romans 12:4–5). As Christians, we need each other. We are to belong together. We are to be interconnected. In this increasingly independent world where 34% of households have only one person living in them,[2] and people have more Facebook friends than they have real friends, it needs effort on our part to ensure that we truly belong to a Christian community.

As I have spent most of the last fifteen years in London, I have seen the increasing tendency for people to view church like a petrol station. We come from our homes to church to refill our spiritual tanks. There happen to be other people on the forecourt filling up their tanks too, but there's no need to get too involved with them. We see church as an individual activity: we drive in, fill up and drive out, and then go back to our independent life.

As I have spent most of the last fifteen years in London, I have seen the increasing tendency for people to view church like a petrol station.

Others see church as an all-you-can-eat buffet. We take the amazing worship from one church, the powerful ministry times from another, the fun singles ministry from a third, and then we listen to the deep teaching of some brilliant preacher on the internet. It may all be very helpful – but it is not church! Being a Christian is about belonging to a community of believers.

As we belong together, so we can build together as we build each other up using our different gifts:

We have different gifts, according to the grace given to each of us. If your gift is prophesying, then prophesy in accordance with your faith; if it is serving, then serve; if it is teaching, then teach; if it is to encourage, then give encouragement; if it is giving, then

give generously; if it is to lead, do it diligently; if it is to show
mercy, do it cheerfully.
(Romans 12:6–8)

In 2012, I moved to Holy Trinity Clapham with around fifty
people from Holy Trinity Brompton, grafting into the wonderful existing congregation that was already there under the
inspired leadership of the Rector, David Isherwood. One of
the things that I was most fascinated by was the reasons that
people gave for wanting to come and be a part of a more local
church. There was the desire, as I expected, to be part of a
smaller church where it was easier to feel like it was a genuine
community due to the church family being in the hundreds
rather than the thousands in numbers. However, there was
also a significant desire to be part of a church where there
was a greater need for individuals to use the different gifts that
God has given them. It has been deeply thrilling to see people
developing and growing in their faith as there have been
increasing opportunities and needs for them to step out and
use their gifts in ways that they haven't done before.

Our relationship with other Christians is to be one of belonging together, building together and also behaving together:

> Love must be sincere. Hate what is evil; cling to what is good. Be
> devoted to one another in brotherly love. Honour one another above
> yourselves. Never be lacking in zeal, but keep your spiritual fervour,
> serving the Lord. Be joyful in hope, patient in affliction, faithful in
> prayer. Share with God's people who are in need. Practise hospitality.
> (Romans 12:9–13)

As Christians, it is vital we are part of a church community
and not isolated. Obviously, believing together is important
– there's no point being part of a church that is not teaching

the 100% gospel. And yet that is not enough. The local church needs to be a place where, in the midst of all the struggles and the stresses and the sinfulness and the stubbornness, there is a desire to belong, build and behave together. As Christians relating to Christians, our relationships should be trans-formed. They should be relationships of *interdependence rather than independence*.

Our relationship with the world transformed

Our relationships with the world should become focused on *love rather than revenge*, even to our enemies. In whatever setting we find people who make our lives a misery, be it church or work or anywhere else, Paul encourages us to show love. He says, 'Do not repay anyone evil for evil . . . Do not take revenge, my dear friends . . . Do not be overcome by evil, but overcome evil with good' (Romans 12:17–21).

It's the same in our relationship to the world of govern-ment. We may not agree with every policy the government pushes through, we may not like the character of a particular politician, but we are to show them love rather than revenge. We are to submit to their leadership, respect them, pay all the taxes we owe and pray for those in authority (Romans 13:1–7).

It's the same with our neighbours. Whether it is our literal neighbours, whose music comes through the wall into our flat at a far greater volume than we would like, or our neigh-bour at work who sits in the adjacent desk, or our neighbour on the train during our daily commute, we are to love them rather than show revenge – even if they shoved past us to get the last seat on the train before us: '"Love your neighbour as yourself." Love does no harm to its neighbour' (Romans 13:9–10 NIV 1984).

Our romantic relationships transformed

I am not the best person to be giving romantic advice. The ineptitude I showed on my first date with my wife Susannah is something of a legend among my friends. I invited her on a romantic picnic in the year 2000. We went to Vauxhall Park which, with no disrespect, is possibly not the most romantic location in the world. Or even in Vauxhall.

I bought the food and drink but then realized that I didn't have a picnic basket. I therefore decided to use my laundry basket, by removing all my smelly socks and boxer shorts, and placing a tea towel on the bottom. We got to Vauxhall Park, complete with laundry basket, and I produced the baguette and fine smoked ham, only to discover that Susannah hates ham. I swiftly moved on to the strawberries. They had gone mouldy.

I carried on regardless, and was desperately trying to pluck up the courage to ask her out, but I was so nervous that I needed a pee. I had to go and hide in the bushes for a pee and a prayer, and brace myself to pop the question. Not the marriage question, just: 'Would you be my girlfriend?'

She said yes – which was very nice, and rather surprising. Then we had a prayer and a kiss. Susannah reckons we prayed before we kissed. I reckon it was the other way round. The jury is still out on that one. But we carried on chatting until late. Then we went to the gates of Vauxhall Park, only to discover that we had been locked in.

Susannah, young gazelle that she is, climbed up the gate and jumped over onto the pavement. I climbed up, but managed to get stuck on top of the gate. Susannah had to climb back up to rescue me. It was a bit like Hugh Grant and Julia Roberts in *Notting Hill*, but in reverse.

So I'm not a great model on the dating front. But more crucially, I'm not hugely successful in terms of godly romantic relationships either. As a teenager, I had a year of being a complete snogmonster. As a young Christian, aged eighteen, I went out with someone for three months who wasn't a Christian, which I wouldn't advise. She was a lovely person, but because I wanted Jesus to be at the centre of my life and he wasn't even in her life, we had different outlooks on life and different expectations for relationships. Over the years, there were times when I was too intimate in some of my romantic relationships. Susannah and I are now in our second decade of married life, and we are not some ideal Christian couple who have never had an argument. We've argued, too much, sometimes heatedly.

So it's a good thing that I can write from a biblical perspective on how God can transform our romantic relationships, rather than from a personal 'Aren't I holy?' stance. I have made many mistakes in the area of romantic relationships. But I am also someone who knows the amazing wonder of complete forgiveness, because Jesus Christ has paid the price of all my sin – a forgiveness that isn't an excuse to carry on sinning, but one that does offer me a fresh start. As Paul writes, 'Let us behave decently, as in the daytime, not in orgies and drunkenness, not in sexual immorality and debauchery, not in dissension and jealousy. Rather, clothe yourselves with the Lord Jesus Christ, and do not think about how to gratify the desires of the sinful nature' (Romans 13:13–14 NIV 1984).

First, it is worth reminding ourselves that we are **social beings**.[3] We have seen as Christians that we are not to be independent, but interdependent, yet actually this is not just a facet of being a Christian, it is also a facet of being human. So think back to the creation account. Again and again there is the refrain that 'it was good', until God says, 'It is not good for the man to be alone' (Genesis 2:18). Here is Adam – in the wonder of paradise, in perfect relationship with God – and something is not good. I've sometimes got this wrong in the past. I've said something like, 'If we're in a right relationship with God, then that's all we ultimately need – everything is OK', but the reality is that Adam was in a right relationship with God and it was not enough. As humans, we need to be in relationship with others as well as in relationship with God. It is not good to live as an isolated individual with a personal relationship with God.

Of course, Genesis 2:18 has more than just romantic relationships in view, but certainly not less. It is right that there should be among us huge compassion for those people who feel that real ache of singleness and the pain of not being married. The Bible doesn't turn its back on singleness, but it understands that ache. We need to recognize and support people who are experiencing that ache. Too often, churches can be so focused on the family – the marrieds, the children – that those who are single feel excluded and on the periphery, and that should not be the case.

We need to recognize the challenge of singleness for many, but also encourage people to see that singleness, when lived out in the context of many healthy friendships, is objectively a good thing. For some single people, it can even feel a good thing. As Paul notes, it is much easier for the unmarried person (like Paul himself) to live a life of 'undivided devotion to the Lord' (see 1 Corinthians 7:32–35).

Second, we are **sexual beings**. Our sexuality is part of who we are. Sex is good. Paul doesn't urge us not to think about gratifying our sexual desires, but not to 'think about how to gratify the desires of the sinful nature' (Romans 13:14 NIV 1984). Sex is only sinful when it takes place in the wrong context, and so we need to be clear on that context.

The blueprint for all the teaching on sex in the Bible is Genesis 2:24: 'For this reason a man will leave his father and

mother and be united to his wife, and they will become one
flesh' (NIV 1984). It's an interesting verse because, of course,
Adam and Eve didn't have any father and mother. It wasn't
relevant to them. Rather, the writer of Genesis wrote this
verse to teach all who would read the book of Genesis. Indeed,
Jesus and Paul both quote Genesis 2:24 in the context of
teaching about sex and marriage – Jesus in Mark 10:7 and Paul
in Ephesians 5:31. This blueprint verse tells us very clearly that
the order is: 1) leave the parents, 2) be united as husband and
wife, 3) become one flesh – have sex. Sex is to be in the context
of marriage.

This context makes sense because intimacy always goes
with commitment in the Bible. It would be deeply offensive
to Jesus if we were to pray,
'Jesus, I want to know intimacy
with you. I want you living in
me by your Spirit; I want you
to lead me and love me. But
I don't want a commitment. I
don't want to forsake all others
and follow you alone. I don't
want to be vulnerable with you. I want to be able to make my
own decisions most of the time.' That is an awful prayer.

Intimacy and commitment must always be connected.

Intimacy and commitment must always be connected. It
works like that in our relationship with God, and it works the
same way in our romantic relationships. Sex (intimacy) is to
be in the context of marriage (commitment). And now, more
than ever, it is important to emphasize that Jesus defined
marriage as being between one man and one woman. For
example, in Mark 10:6–7, he explicitly links 'God made them
male and female' (Genesis 1:27) with our blueprint verse.
Jesus joins the affirmation of humanity as male and female
in Genesis 1:27 with the affirmation of exclusive uniting

through sex in marriage in Genesis 2:24. Jesus says that sex is to be in the context of marriage between one man and one woman.

Of course I am not saying it is easy to keep sex for marriage between husband and wife. Of course I am not saying there is no forgiveness when we muck up. Of course I am not saying we should countenance any form of homophobia in the church.[4] Yet we cannot ignore God's teaching when it comes to thinking through the place for sex, how we date, and faithfulness in marriage.

Third, we are **spiritual beings**. G. K. Chesterton famously said that 'every man who knocks on the door of a brothel is looking for God'. We're all looking for perfect love, for complete intimacy, for unconditional acceptance. Neither a prostitute, nor a spouse, nor any other human can ever perfectly provide these things. Yet many of us find ourselves idolizing a particular person, or worshipping sex or marriage, rather than worshipping God.

For the single person, it can lead to being too choosy in evaluating potential marriage prospects, not realizing that we are inevitably going to marry someone with whom we're going to have disagreements; after all, it is one sinner married to another sinner. It can also mean we fail to enjoy life as a single person. We think that marriage will save us from all the isolation and the loneliness and the struggles we face. The feelings of loneliness are real and understandable and often very painful, but the truth is that marriage will not solve them. In fact, the loneliest people in life are often not those who are single, but those who are in unhappy marriages. Jesus is our Saviour. Not marriage.

For the married person, if we are worshipping our spouse or marriage, rather than God, then life will prove difficult because we won't be able to handle the frustrations of marriage. I know I've been guilty of this at times. I have ended up placing completely unreasonable demands on Susannah. I can't expect her to provide me with the perfect love, complete intimacy and unconditional acceptance that I desire. She's pretty amazing, but she is not God!

The solution to this problem of idolatry is not to love other people less; it is to love Jesus more. As Paul writes, 'Clothe yourselves with the Lord Jesus Christ' (Romans 13:14). We need to be more taken up with love for Jesus, and clothe ourselves with him. We are to be focused on *long-term commitment, rather than short-term gratification.*

The motive for transformed relationships

The book of Romans is the biggest and longest and most meaty of all of Paul's letters in the New Testament. Yet in Romans 12:1, he summarizes the first eleven chapters in one phrase: 'in view of God's mercy'.

Those five words are the motive for Christian living in a nutshell. They transform all our relationships: with ourselves, other Christians, our neighbours, our government and our romantic connections. Yet these transformed relationships are deeply challenging. It is a challenge, in relating to ourselves, to be humble rather than proud; in relating to other Christians, to be interdependent rather than independent; in relating to the world, to be loving, not seeking revenge; and in relating romantically, to be focused on long-term commitment rather than short-term gratification. So why bother?

The answer in each case is: 'in view of God's mercy'. What we first receive is always and only the motive for how we respond. The only reason we might either desire or be enabled to be a 'red tower' Christian, looking to live out the gospel in all of life, is because of what God has mercifully first done for us, sending Jesus to die for us and sending the Spirit to live in us.

So I should look to be humble rather than proud, in view of God's mercy. I don't deserve to be a Christian. I didn't earn my salvation. It's not my good works but Christ's good work on the cross that saved me. I've got no reason to be proud.

I should be interdependent with other Christians rather than independent, in view of God's mercy. God didn't need me. He could have remained independent but, in his mercy, he reached out to me. As Jesus reached out his hands on the cross, it's as though he was reaching out to me, letting me know that despite all I had done, I could experience God's mercy for myself.

I should bother showing love rather than revenge to the world, even to my enemies, in view of God's mercy. After all, when I was God's enemy, God didn't seek revenge and punishment. He showed me love by dying for me.

I should bother showing long-term commitment rather than short-term gratification in my romantic relationships, in view of God's mercy. Jesus gave up his life in love for me. He didn't need to show me unconditional love, but in his mercy, he did. As he went to the cross, he was focused on long-term commitment rather than short-term gratification.

Not everyone gets the opportunity to say 'I will' in marriage. However, we all have the opportunity to say 'I will' to Jesus. He is the only one who can really save us and give us perfect love and complete affirmation. He is the ultimate spouse. We can look up to him and his mercy, and we can look forward to the ultimate wedding day: 'Our salvation is nearer now than when we first believed. The night is nearly over; the day is almost here' (Romans 13:11–12). The day that is nearing is actually a wedding day – a wedding between Christians and Jesus. In fact, the Bible starts with a wedding day in Genesis 2, and finishes with a wedding day in Revelation 19. On that final wedding day, we can fall into Jesus' merciful arms, knowing that this is the one marital relationship that will last for ever.

100% activation

I struggle every day to offer my body as a living sacrifice, holy and pleasing to God. If I took this more seriously I wonder whether I would consume the same foods and avoid exercise in quite the same way? My complaints about lines, marks and dark circles show my dissatisfaction with what is increasingly a middle-aged woman's body (aargh!). While I can use a bit of foundation to make things appear more pleasing to the eye, it is perhaps what happens within that is harder to cover up, especially from God.

While I wish that I could say I do not conform to the patterns of this world, sadly their appeal is often just too great and I'm drawn to quick fixes on the exterior rather than addressing what is unseen. I pray every day, 'Please, Lord, renew my mind!' I know alone I cannot do it. I keep going back to Paul's words in Romans 7:15: 'I do not understand what I do. For what I want to do I do not do, but what I hate I do.' I'm in good company.

When it comes to relationships, they are the easiest and hardest part of my life. I once had a job role titled 'Relationship Manager', which seemed a bit ironic, as I was often struggling in this area. While relationships with people not close to me are very easy to sustain, it has always been those within the inner circle that have been trickier. I like to think that since coming to Christ in 2007 I have worked harder at those relationships, but I know that I have very often failed. The problem is that the first relationship to be transformed is the one with ourselves, and that is where time and again I fall down.

Community is the saving grace. However, for someone like me, it can also be a minefield. I live on my own and could be described as 'fiercely independent'. I like seeing friends – when I want to – and I like community, mainly when it's convenient for me. My Bible seems to be telling me something different about community, which is why I keep trying to get better at the 'group thing'. It may be because I'm scared of being held to account or getting too deep into something I can't get out of, but with my flight mentality, a red light often flashes when invited to a Christian's home for 'fellowship time'.

The big stumbling block is romantic relationships. OK – so I'm a self-confessed Bridget Jones. I have a huge back catalogue of dating disaster stories. I don't know whether I have any wisdom to offer, but the only thing that I do know for sure is there is no condemnation in Christ, that he loves us completely and that I want to be better for him. I would love to be married, and I rant and rage against God about being thirty-four and single. I mean, surely this was never meant to be me? However, it is. While there are many lonely and frustrating moments, I trust that God has the master plan, and I reckon it's got to be better than anything I'd come up with.

(Nicola Saunders, not-for-profit development director)

100% adoration

Heavenly Father, in view of your mercy,
I offer my body to you as a living sacrifice
    – this is my spiritual act of worship.
May you transform me by the renewing of my mind,
    so that my relationships may more and more display
       Christ-likeness.

Thank you for that future wedding day when I can fall into
your Son's merciful arms.

In his name I pray.

Amen.

8. Christianity is 100% inter-relational

1) Our relationship with **ourselves** transformed *(12:3)*

Humble, not proud

2) Our relationship with **Christians** transformed *(12:4–13)*

Interdependent, not independent

3) Our relationship with **the world** transformed *(12:14 – 13:10)*

Love, not revenge

4) Our relationship with **romantic interests** transformed *(13:11–14)*

Long-term commitment, not short-term gratification

Why bother? *'In view of **God's mercy**' (12:1–2)*

100% application

1. 'I am not what I ought to be . . . I am not what I wish to be . . . I am not what I hope to be . . . Yet . . . I can truly say, I am not what I once was.' How do you relate to these words?
2. Do you view church like a petrol station, an all-you-can-eat buffet, or is it a Christian community where you belong, build and behave with other Christians?

3. Do you know, and do you live in the light of, the liberating wonder of complete forgiveness from Jesus for all your sexual sin?

4. At the moment, are you idolizing a particular person, or sex, or marriage, rather than idolizing God?

Read Romans 12 – 13.

9. CHRISTIANITY IS 100% INTEGRATED

(Romans 14 – 16)

> For everything that was written in the past was written to
> teach us, so that through endurance and the encouragement
> of the Scriptures we might have hope. May the God who
> gives endurance and encouragement give you a spirit of
> unity among yourselves as you follow Christ Jesus, so that
> with one heart and mouth you may glorify the God and
> Father of our Lord Jesus Christ.
> (Romans 15:4–6 NIV 1984)

The previous chapter finished with the greatest wedding that
will ever be conducted. This chapter starts with some weddings
that haven't been conducted so well. As you may know, when
you get married in a church, as long as the vicar has said the
declarations: 'Will you take So-and-so to be your husband/
wife . . .', and the bride and groom have replied, 'I will', then,
once the paperwork has been signed, it is a legal wedding.

This is a good thing – because I seem to have a habit of,
by mistake, missing bits out of weddings that I conduct.
Thankfully I haven't missed out the declarations. But one
couple had spent ages choosing their hymns for the big day,
only for me to miss out completely one hymn on the Order
of Service. For another, the family situation meant that it was

really important for the father of the bride to declare his blessing and desire for the marriage to be taking place. Unfortunately, I then forgot to ask the question, 'Who gives this woman to be married to this man?' My dear friends Ross and Anna Arnold didn't tell me until months afterwards, but at their wedding I forgot to do the bit where the vicar takes the right hand of both the bride and groom and holds them up, declaring to the congregation the words of Jesus: 'Those whom God has joined together, let no one put asunder' (see Matthew 19:6).

Now those words meant a particular, important thing when Jesus spoke them, and mean it still when they are repeated in a marriage service. They are a warning given to anyone about getting in the way of the stability and security of a married couple, by encouraging the couple to pull apart from each other, perhaps through flirtatious advances. God has joined together two individuals in marriage, and no-one should try to pull them apart.

Those words are true for marriage, but they are also true for many other things. When it comes to Christianity and the good news about Jesus, so often Christians are in danger of putting asunder – pulling apart, dis-integrating – what God has meant to stay joined together.[1]

1. In terms of our doctrine, we are to *personalize* and *globalize* the gospel

At the very centre of the gospel is a personal message of salvation to each one of us. The key verse of the whole letter of Romans is: 'I am not ashamed of the gospel, because it is the power of God for the salvation of everyone who believes' (Romans 1:16 NIV 1984). Paul recognizes the personal nature of this message of salvation – it is for every individual who believes. Again, he says that 'if you confess with your mouth, "Jesus is Lord," and believe in your heart that God raised him from the dead, you will be saved' (Romans 10:9 NIV 1984). It is deeply personal. Will you and I repent and believe the good news that Christ died for us in our place?

And yet the danger is that I can end up putting myself and my needs at the very centre of the gospel, rather than ensuring Jesus Christ is at the centre. Our doctrine needs to be integrated, so we understand that the gospel is deeply personal, but is also truly global. The two go together. They mustn't be put asunder. It's not just about my believing in Jesus so I go to heaven when I die.

It's about becoming part of a new global kingdom, with King Jesus in charge. Everything is moving towards this new perfect kingdom – a new heaven and a new earth. Not just me or you, but the whole globe. In Romans 8, we discovered that we, as Christians, are groaning as we wait for our own redemption, but also that the whole creation has been groaning as in the pains of childbirth.

When we have an integrated doctrine that keeps the personal and the global elements of the gospel together, then it leads to an **Integrated Mindset**. Jesus is seen to be Lord of everything in this world, and everything in our lives. There's no area outside his remit. Abraham Kuyper, the Dutch theologian, famously declared, 'There is not one square inch of this world over which Jesus Christ does not cry, "This is mine."'[2] The gospel is not about me turning up to church for an hour on Sunday and serving on the occasional rota. It is not about me praying a prayer of commitment and then keeping on living my life as normal with a midweek Bible study group for entertainment. God is changing the entire world and he calls us to be a part of his work.

Furthermore, we can be about this work in whatever sphere we find ourselves. So Martin Luther once wrote:

> It is pure fiction that Pope, bishops, priests, and monks are called the 'spiritual estate' while princes, lords, artisans and farmers are called the 'temporal estate'. This is indeed a piece of deceit . . . all Christians are truly of the spiritual estate, and there is no difference among them except that of office.[3]

Having this Integrated Mindset means we see that we can be living for Jesus and making a difference for him in all areas of life. It's not just about how I am involved at church, but how I am living for Jesus, working for his goals, transforming things in his name throughout the whole of life. You – in and through your workplace, your sports team, your pub, your university, your community centre, your street, your family – can be a part of God's work in this world. This is the 'red tower' life.

2. In terms of our declaration of Jesus, we are to *proclaim* and *demonstrate* the gospel

It is absolutely vital that the good news of Jesus is communicated with words. We must be people with 'beautiful feet', speaking the good news of Jesus. As Paul comes to the conclusion of his letter, he says that he has the 'duty of proclaiming the gospel of God' (Romans 15:16), and that 'it has always been [his] ambition to preach the gospel' (15:20).

And yet, in this conclusion, he also says that he 'will not venture to speak of anything except what Christ has accomplished through me in leading the Gentiles to obey God by what I have *said and done* – by the power of signs and wonders, through the power of the Spirit of God' (Romans 15:18–19, my italics). As well as declaring Jesus through our words, we are also to declare Jesus through our actions, and through amazing works of the Spirit. Words, works and wonders are all together in our declaration of Jesus to others. Proclamation and demonstration should not be pulled apart from each other.

Words are primary. Without them, no-one will hear of Jesus. But we are to have words integrated with actions, evidence integrated with experience, proclamation integrated with demonstration. This integrated declaration leads to an **Integrated Mission**. Our evangelism is to have a social dimension, and our social action is to have an evangelistic dimension.

Take a typical church fête with kids on the bouncy castle, old ladies buzzing round the flower stall, cakes by the thousand, and the vicar grimly determined to knock a coconut down at the coconut shy. If the motive for a church fête is to merely raise a bit of money for the church, then it probably wouldn't be worth doing it. But if a church uses its fête to connect with the community and encourage people to connect with the life of the church, and supremely with Jesus, then it is a more than worthwhile endeavour. The social action and the evangelism need to be intertwined.

The mission of the church looking out is to be integrated, but so too is the mission of the church looking in. A church where there is internal dis-integration is a disaster. This was particularly an issue for the early church in Rome as there were obviously deep divisions between Jewish and non-Jewish Christians. The church was in danger of dis-integrating. Paul writes, 'One person's faith allows them to eat anything, but another, whose faith is weak, eats only vegetables . . . One person considers one day more sacred than another; another considers every day alike' (Romans 14:2, 5). Most likely, both of these issues were disagreements along Jewish–Gentile lines, with the Jewish and Jewish-influenced Christians thinking that they should still be careful only to eat kosher meat. Because you couldn't be sure what you were eating from the Roman equivalent of Tesco, they thought the safest option was to be a vegetarian. Similarly, the Jewish Christians thought it right to continue keeping the Jewish festivals, while the Gentile Christians saw them as neither necessary nor beneficial.

Now these subjects under discussion may not be so relevant to us today, and it is relatively unimportant which side was right. The key is that these two issues were leading to the dis-integration of the church. Both sides saw themselves as superior to the other (Romans 14:3). Rather than unity and integrity among the Christians in Rome, there was judgmentalism, fuelled by endless debates and argument. So often, it is the same today.

When you think about it, it's inevitable. When Susannah and I got married, we chose each other, and there were just two of us, and yet we had all manner of arguments and difficulties to begin with. Twelve years on, we are not immune from an argument. If that is what happens for two people *choosing* to come together, it is no wonder that there is disagreement and argument when lots of Christians (plus some people who probably aren't Christians) come together in a local church, or when lots of local churches and denominations come together with each other. Unlike Susannah and me, Christians don't choose each other. We choose Christ, but we don't choose our brothers and sisters in Christ. In many ways, it is hardly surprising that the church often resembles a bickering, dis-integrated family.

It is into this situation that Paul pleads for an end to the dis-integration of the church, and there are three main motives that he gives for Jew and Gentile, 'weak' and 'strong', to be united and integrated together.[4]

First, our motivation for integration and unity among Christians is the cross. We are to 'accept one another, then, just as Christ accepted [us]' (Romans 15:7). The only reason we are accepted by God is because of the cross. We don't deserve to be accepted by Jesus, but he does accept us. We should have the same attitude with other Christians – accepting them rather than judging, despising or condemning those whom Jesus also died to save.

Second, our motivation is the resurrection. It is because Jesus rose from the dead that he is Lord (Romans 14:9). We are therefore to live as ones who belong to the Lord (14:8), and are therefore accountable to him as our Master as to how we live. He doesn't want us judging our Christian brothers and sisters (14:10a), and so out of obedience to him we should look to be unified.

Third, our motivation is Christ's return. We will all have to give an account of ourselves to God. He will judge us, so for us to presume to stand in judgment of other Christians is for us to try to take the place of Jesus (Romans 14:10–12).

Today, the debates in the church that are causing disintegration are likely not to be about the merits of vegetables, and they are rarely about the place of the Sabbath as a special day. But the principle here is still vitally relevant. The area that affects me most is the debate between conservative and charismatic Christians. When I moved from working at the more conservative All Souls, Langham Place to the more charismatic Holy Trinity Brompton, I had brothers and sisters in Christ from both 'tribes' looking down in judgment at me – though not, I hasten to add, anyone in leadership of either church. 'You've finally broken free of the shackles of All Souls to experience the Spirit,' said one person at HTB. 'You can put our charismatic friends straight on a few things.' said one person at All Souls. Yet Paul says we are not to 'judge', 'look down on' or 'condemn' our fellow Christians who think differently from us (Romans 14:10, 22 NIV 1984).

Whether it is between the Jewish Christians and the Gentile Christians back in Rome, or whether it is between different factions of Christians today, disunity is so destructive. That is why Paul prays as he does for the church in Rome: 'May the God who gives endurance and encouragement give you a spirit of unity among yourselves as you follow Christ Jesus, so that with one heart and mouth you may glorify the God and Father of our Lord Jesus Christ' (Romans 15:5–6 NIV 1984).

And yet unity with the gospel is even more vital than unity with other people. When Paul is urging unity in the Roman church despite disagreements over the eating of meat and the importance of special days, he refers to these debates as 'disputable matters' (Romans 14:1). However, it is a very different situation with a matter that is 'indisputable' – supremely clear matters at the core of the gospel which determine how we get right with God. Think of Paul's words to the church in Galatia. He declared, 'If anybody is preaching to you a gospel other than what you accepted, let [them] be eternally condemned!' (Galatians 1:9 NIV 1984). On an indisputable gospel matter, unity with the gospel must win over unity with the person.

In the sixteenth century, two great theologians, Luther and Erasmus, were having a debate. At one point Luther said to Erasmus, 'The difference between you and me, Erasmus, is that you sit above Scripture and judge it, while I sit under Scripture and let it judge me.'[5] I don't know if Luther's assessment of Erasmus was correct (I'll leave that judgment to the church historians), but Luther's point is certainly a good one.

Truly united, integrated Christian communities exist, not where everyone sits in judgment over the Bible and can decide whatever they like, but rather where people are ready together to sit under the authority of the Scriptures. Paul reminds the Christians in Rome of this. It is when they are sitting under the Scriptures that they can know a spirit of unity as they follow Jesus (Romans 15:4–5).

Whether the focus is on looking out at those outside the church community, or whether it is looking in at those within it, the authority of Scripture is key to an integrated mission where what is proclaimed in words matches what is also demonstrated in actions. We often read that Jesus prayed, but the Bible rarely tells us in detail what he prayed – with one exception. In John's Gospel, Jesus prays, 'May they be brought to complete unity to let the world know that you sent me and have loved them even as you have loved me' (John 17:23b NIV 1984). An integrated church community is part of the integrated church mission.

3. In terms of our discipleship, we are to *believe* and *live* the gospel

As Christians, we can get into the danger of separating the belief of faith from the life of faith. So long as we have prayed the right prayer, then we think it doesn't really matter how we live our life. Of course, as the letter of Romans shows best of all, we are saved only by the work of Jesus on the cross for us – and through faith in that work. We are not saved by us doing good works. Yet a genuine faith will always demonstrate itself in obedience to God (Romans 1:5; 15:18; 16:26). Our discipleship must be integrated: believing and living the gospel go together.

It may not be too grand a claim to say that the group of Christians that best exemplify this integration of believing and living in the last 300 years are the 'Clapham sect', who worshipped at Holy Trinity Clapham, the church where I now work. Led by William Wilberforce, the politician and committed Christian who worked for the abolition of the slave trade, they transformed their community, their country and the world for the cause of Christ. They were a varied group, including bankers, poets, editors and a brewer, as well as politicians and, of course, a vicar. If the Clapham sect were a band (which as far as I know they weren't), Wilberforce was undoubtedly the front man of the group – the lead singer. However, the drummer, the one keeping them on track and on beat, was the rector of Holy Trinity Clapham at the time, John Venn. And this, a quote from one of his sermons, was the beat to which they marched:

> Religion is not merely an act of homage paid upon our bended knees to God; it is not confined to the closet and the church, nor is it restrained to the hours of the Sabbath; it is a general principle extended to a person's whole conduct in every transaction and in every place. I know no mistake which is more dangerous than that which lays down devotional feelings alone as the test of true religion . . . Till our Christianity appears in our conversation, in our business, in our pleasures, in the aims and objects of our life, we have not attained to a conformity to the image of our Saviour, nor have we learned his Gospel aright.[6]

It is this beat that, for both the Clapham sect, and for you and me, will lead to an **Integrated Me**.

John Venn didn't have this luxury, but at Holy Trinity Clapham today I will often have a hands-free microphone headset on for the whole service. It's affectionately known as the 'Britney mic' in honour of the famous pop princess. However, this update since 1800 has led to problems, when those on the production desk have failed to mute my microphone when I am not actually supposed to be heard.

One Sunday, very early in my time at the church, one old lady came up to me at the end of a service and said, 'How can I put this politely? Would you turn off your microphone during the songs? It rather spoils the service for everyone else.' I understood where she was coming from (see chapter 2 and the story of the junior choir). With the Britney mic, I was oblivious to the fact that what I thought was very much a personal experience of me warbling out the songs was actually a highly integrated experience for the rest of the church.

But at least that was better than what happened to a friend of mine. He and his wife were round at someone's house for supper. They'd taken their baby with them, along with a travel cot, and they'd put the baby to sleep in a bedroom. During pudding they heard the baby crying over the baby monitor, and they went to sort her out, and chatted to each other in the bedroom about how the conversation over supper was pretty boring, and they should try to make a quick getaway. Back in the kitchen, their hosts were hearing this discussion loud and clear over the baby monitor. It led to rather an awkward entry into the kitchen when they returned.

It is so easy to become so focused on ourselves and our own little worlds that we end up living a dis-integrated life. That can go undetected for years, until suddenly, just as with the Britney mic or the baby monitor, the disconnect is made public for all to see. As is commonly said, 'Integrity is doing the right thing, even when no-one is watching.'

We have all heard of stories in the media where there has been a 'credibility gap' between the words and the actions of a church leader. Yet, while we may not have personally made

the errors that these individuals have, none of us can sit comfortably. So often, there is dis-integration between our public
lives and our private lives, or between what we profess and
what we practise.

All of us have heroes in the Christian faith. Your heroes will
be different from mine, but I would wager that one of the key
ingredients in making them heroes in each case is their
integrity. We are attracted by the fact that, in their life, what
you see is what you get.

So I think of John Stott, my number one twentieth- and
twenty-first-century hero. John Stott was the pastor, theologian
and evangelical statesman, whose parish was the world and
whose home was All Souls, Langham Place. He died in 2011.
He was someone whom I had the privilege of calling a
colleague for five years. He felt like my spiritual grandfather.

Through his writings, he has made a greater impression on
me than any other author outside the Bible. And yet the reason
why he is my hero is not so much because of his writings, but
because of the integrity that I witnessed when I knew him. In
the conclusion of a book that is a portrait of the man by his
friends, this is the picture that is given: 'Like a seaside stick of
rock, he was the same all the way through. It seemed that,
wherever you might break him open, the lettering would be the
same: the message of his life and his words was consistent.'[7]

Or I think of William Wilberforce, my number one eight-
eenth- and nineteenth-century hero. His passion for Christ
and to make a difference in this world is inspiring. His zeal for
the abolition of the slave trade was phenomenal. And yet it is
the integrity of Wilberforce that has made the greatest impression upon me as I have investigated his life. His honesty about
his struggles, his passion to be more like Christ, his impressive
manner as a husband and father, his attitude to money and
possessions, the use of his time, the high importance he placed

on resting as well as working hard – it is all this evidence of
his integrity that has had the biggest impact upon me. It seems
to have had the same effect on one of his biographers, William
Hague, the UK Foreign Secretary. Hague's masterful
biography of Wilberforce concludes with these final sentences:
'Wilberforce's pursuit of a broad and uplifting vision of
society elevates him far above the general ranks of politicians.
But the fact that he managed to live according to his own
principles, and constantly reflect his beliefs in his own character, is his crowning glory.'[8] Personal integrity is the hallmark
of the individual Christian. The Integrated Me is to be our
aim and our desire.

It may be our aim, yet the reality is that it is so easy to be a
hypocrite. I can look so calm at work on the outside, but inside
I'm a bundle of worry and anxiety. I may seem a picture of
marital bliss on the outside when I turn up for supper with
some friends, but internally I'm furious with Susannah
because we've just had a disagreement. At times I appear a
fine upstanding church leader on the outside, but inside my
heart is actually cold, apathetic and indifferent towards
my Lord. It's easy to fool people for a while, and yet it is so
difficult to have thoughts and actions that truly match.

I love the story of Bernard of Clairvaux, the twelfth-
century French monk. He mentored Bernard of Pisa, who
became Pope Eugene III. However, Bernard was concerned
about whether Eugene had enough integrity, and whether,
with the responsibility of being Pope, he could keep his public
life and his private life together. As a result, he counselled
Eugene as follows: 'Remove yourself from the demands, lest
you be distracted and get a hard heart. If you are not terrified
by it, it is yours already.'[9]

There have been several times in my life when I have really
lost that integration. For me it is nearly always the result of

two combined problems: being too busy and not spending enough time in prayer. I think, just recently, of my first year working at Holy Trinity Clapham. I was in a new job, with new responsibilities, leading a new venture of integrating a group of people from one church into another existing church and starting up a new weekly evening service. My preaching, diplomacy, management and pastoral skills have been, and continue to be, stretched in all directions, sometimes beyond breaking point. I have never had to work harder in my life. And in the busyness, while outwardly things went fairly well, inwardly my prayer life was squeezed, my impatience flared more frequently with my long-suffering family, and I became more hardened in my relationship with Christ. Susannah had to challenge me rather vociferously about it for me to recognize the spiritual dangers that I was in.

As Bernard recommended to Eugene, and as Susannah recommended to me, what is needed above all in these times is to remove ourselves from all the demands for long enough to recalibrate ourselves with God, and not let whatever is occupying all our time distract us from our primary responsibility of nurturing our own relationship with him. We need to rekindle our relationships with Christ in the quiet of prayer and reading his Word. In his excellent book, *The Emotionally Healthy Church*, Pete Scazzero comments,

> When our life *with* God is not sufficient to sustain our work *for* God, we too will find ourselves struggling with our integrity . . . work *for* God that is not nourished by a deep interior life *with* God will eventually be contaminated. Our experiential sense of worth and validation gradually shifts from God's love for us in Christ to our works and performance. The joy of life with Christ slowly, almost imperceptibly, disappears.[10]

Wherever it is that you are working for God – in your work place and your church, among your friends and community and family – it will only be viable in the long term when it is fuelled by your life with God.

The Integrated Me is a tough call. It is something that will always be a challenge throughout our earthly lives. And yet we must keep our focus on it and continuously make room for God's Spirit to convict us and reconstruct us, so that our hearts are not hard, and so our private and public lives match. We cannot fulfil our purpose as God's creatures when we are living dis-integrated lives.

There is a Thomas the Tank Engine cartoon that pictures Thomas, on his side, having fallen off the train tracks. He's shouting, 'I'm free! I'm free at last. I've fallen off the rails and I'm free!' Of course, the reality is that Thomas is far more 'free' when his wheels are on the rails and he is operating in line with how he has been created to function. We have been given the secret to making life work. We are to follow our Maker's instructions and be people of integrity, believing and obeying. If we decide to jump off those rails, no wonder disaster and pain and frustration follow. It is the Holy Spirit who picks us up time and again and places us back on the tracks of God's Word, so that you and I might more and more be free to live as an Integrated Me, complete with an Integrated Mindset, and give ourselves to the cause of God's Integrated Mission.

100% activation

When I graduated from university, most of my classmates from Princeton went to New York to work in consulting or banking but I still had an itch to travel. I hadn't taken a gap year, so when the opportunity came up to go to China – and to do so as a missionary under the guise of being a rugby coach – it sounded perfect!

Four long years later, I finally left China. I'd managed to well and truly scratch that travel itch and Shanghai had become my home. I'd picked up some Mandarin, learned how to navigate the packed cycle lanes and, far more importantly, I'd realised a lot of truths about my own faith – and just how it lacked real integration when put to the test.

I'd grown up in a Christian family and gone through my first twenty-or-so years trying to do mostly what I thought I 'should' be doing. Having to explain my faith day in and day out to young Chinese students, hungry to know more, was a different story. Many would go into jobs in the cities nearby and come back to me saying: 'I've told all my colleagues I love Jesus. Now what?'. As amazing as this was, they soon realised that there were other questions at work like: Why shouldn't we fix the books of the firm? Why is it better for the business community not to be based on bribery? How do I respond when my boss wants me to hire prostitutes for the clients? These were tough questions to answer, let alone for very young Christians, and it was amazing to see both them and me wrestle with the answers.

Now that I live back in the more familiar setting of London and work in a management consulting firm, the questions aren't exactly the same, but the need to live out my Christian worldview in an integrated way has many of the same challenges.

My last two years in China were spent working for a Christian who ran his own gift business in America. He taught all his employees, whatever their faith, his business philosophy: that we are here to use the skills we have to make each day better than the last – to be agents of redemption. Of course, and most importantly, this can happen through conversion to Christ, but it can also happen through the jobs we do: helping people express love and connect with the beauty of creation through a wonderful piece of art or a gift; enjoying the world in which we live through the books we read; and even bringing change through helping businesses grow or find efficiencies.

Living out my Christian faith at work is a constant and daily challenge. It's good to get reminders to pick my head up from time to time and make sure that the work I am doing is truly integrated with my faith. Can I explain how my firm is bringing about redemption in the world? What would redemption even look like for my industry?

Beyond work, the integration of my faith in my personal life has often been just as hard for me: rugby teams aren't the best place for sober living! One thing that helps bring up the topic of faith is to have 'launchers' – things that help start a conversation off towards God. In the last few years, that launcher for me has been an active involvement in anti-slavery initiatives.

I studied William Wilberforce at university and on the back of that came face to face with the fact that almost 30 million people are still in slavery or forced labour today. These past few years it's been amazing to work as part of a group of friends who have also caught a vision for change. After some time we managed to commission the Centre for Social Justice to write a comprehensive report on slavery in the UK – and now in 2013 the Home Secretary is standing firmly behind a Modern Slavery Bill as proposed by that report.

Given this campaign, it is certainly inspiring to sit each week in the same church (Holy Trinity Clapham) that Wilberforce, Macaulay, Venn, Thornton and others of the Clapham Group used to attend. But it's even more inspiring to see the church, friends, and others getting involved in this cause and so many others like it – to see faith well and truly in action.

Living my life in a way where my faith is born out in every aspect of what I do, whether at work or at home, will continue to prove challenging – and to be able to look back and around at other examples of integrated living gives well-needed inspiration.

This process of integration is certainly a journey, but I know that we have good examples and the saving grace of a relationship with Christ on our side!
(Cameron Young, mangagement consultant)

100% adoration

May you, the God of hope, fill me with all joy and peace as I trust
    in you,
    so that I may overflow with hope by the power of the Holy Spirit.
In Jesus' name I pray.
Amen.
(Based on Romans 15:13)

9. Christianity is 100% integrated

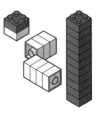

1) **Our doctrine**
Personalize *and* **globalize** the Gospel

Integrated Doctrine	→	Integrated Mindset

2) **Our declaration**
Proclaim *and* **demonstrate** the Gospel

Integrated Declaration	→	Integrated Mission

3) **Our discipleship**
Believe *and* **live** the Gospel

Integrated Discipleship	→	Integrated Me

100% application

1. Who is at the centre of the gospel you believe? You or Jesus? How is this evident?
2. How do you, and the local church you are a part of, measure up in terms of Integrated Mission where words are integrated with actions, evidence is integrated with experience and proclamation is integrated with demonstration?
3. It was said of John Stott, 'Like a seaside stick of rock, he was the same all the way through.' Can that be said of you? In your case, what might the lettering on the stick of rock say?
4. What encouragements have you experienced recently where the Holy Spirit has been picking you up and putting you back on the railtracks of God's Word?

Read Romans 14 – 16.

CONCLUSION: THE CASE OF THE MISSING 'O'

> I have written to you quite boldly on some points, as if to
> remind you of them again, because of the grace God gave
> me to be a minister of Christ Jesus to the Gentiles with the
> priestly duty of proclaiming the gospel of God, so that
> the Gentiles might become an offering acceptable to God,
> sanctified by the Holy Spirit.
>
> (Romans 15:15–16 NIV 1984)

The gospel changes everything. The good news about Jesus
is for *all* of your life. Zero ('o') is missing. Everything is
included. Like the lager, Heineken, the gospel is a worldview
that refreshes the parts other worldviews cannot reach.

First, the good news of Jesus is for all of your life *personally*.
The gospel is not just a series of intellectual propositions, or
a source of emotional highs, or a sequence of mandated tasks.
The gospel speaks to your mind *and* your heart *and* your will.
It interacts with your entire personality. It does this because
Jesus speaks to your mind and your heart and your will. He is
interested in all of you.

Second, the good news about Jesus is for all of your life
compartmentally. The gospel affects how you run your business,
how you drive your car, how you play your football, how you
parent your children, how you respond to what you read in
the newspaper, how you use your free time, how you spend

your money. There is not one area where the gospel does not make a difference, because there is not one area in which Jesus does not make a difference. Jesus is interested in all of you in all of your life.

Third, the good news about Jesus is for all of your life *temporally*. There will never be a time when you don't need Jesus. There will never be a time when you grow out of Jesus, or need to water him down, or put him on the shelf, or pack him away. He is for now, and he will be for ever. Jesus is interested in all of you in all of your life for all time from this moment right into eternity.

One hundred per cent Christianity is not about placing a heavy burden on you, or me, to attempt to guilt us into trying harder to move closer to some magical 100% performance as a Christian. Quite the opposite. It is to remind us that when we receive all the gospel in our minds and hearts and wills, then we are released from having to perform in a certain way or meet a certain standard. It is as we receive all the gospel with all passion in all of life, that we start to respond more and more in joy and out of gratitude for all that Jesus has done for us.

Towards the end of Paul's letter to the Christians in Rome, he speaks of the grace that God gave him to be a minister of Christ Jesus. Everything we have is due to God's grace, and everything we do is in response to God's grace. As William Wilberforce once wrote, 'True Christians consider themselves not as satisfying some rigorous creditor, but as discharging a debt of gratitude.'[1] My prayer is that this book will foster in you a growing gratitude for the gospel in your life, leading to a growing passion to discharge that debt of gratitude throughout all of your life, whoever you are, whatever your age or particular sphere of influence, large or small.

There's an old story of a young boy who was very moved by a sermon he heard in church one Sunday. After the sermon, the offering plate was passed round. The boy saw the plate approaching him, and so looked in his pockets to find a coin to give in response. There was no coin – the case of the missing 'O'. This child had no money to give. In fact, all he could find in his pockets were a conker, a rusty old penknife and a dirty handkerchief, and he didn't feel that any of these were adequate gifts in the light of all that God had given him.

While the boy had been doing all this coin investigation, the offering plate had reached him, and so he stood there, unsure of what to do. He hesitated for a moment while he held the offering plate in his hands, but then he decided on an appropriate course of action. Tentatively he put the offering plate onto the floor in front of his feet. He stepped forwards onto the plate. He decided to offer himself in response to the gospel.

You and I are that boy. We have the same decision to make.

Paul says that his whole aim in proclaiming the gospel was that the Gentiles 'might become an offering acceptable to God, sanctified by the Holy Spirit' (Romans 15:16). That is his desire for you too. Will you step onto the plate and be an offering acceptable to God, sanctified by the Holy Spirit? It means that all of you – including *your* work, *your* talents, *your* relationships, *your* money, *your* time, *your* thought life – is to be placed onto the plate. It means being the tall red tower of Lego, not just a tall white tower with a block of red that can come on or off depending on the circumstances. It means holding nothing back, regardless of what might happen and where God might take you. It means letting God sanctify you and make you holy through the work of his Spirit.

It means your whole life, offered up to God.

After all, he first offered up his whole life for you.

NOTES

Introduction: The case of the missing 'O'

1. These are both great courses which help people to investigate and explore the Christian faith.
2. If you want to read a commentary on Romans, two suggestions are: John Stott, *The Message of Romans: God's Good News for the World*, The Bible Speaks Today (IVP, 1994) (smaller) and Douglas Moo, *The Epistle to the Romans* (Eerdmans, 1996) (larger).

Part 1 100% gospel

1. I originally heard a phrase along these lines from David Jackman on the Cornhill Training Course.

Chapter 1 Christianity is 100% Christ

1. Quoted in John Stott, *The Message of Romans: God's Good News for the World*, The Bible Speaks Today (IVP, 1994), p. 49.
2. The word 'gospel' (*evangelion* in Greek) literally means 'good news'.
3. Quoted in John Stott, *The Incomparable Christ* (IVP, 2001), p. 15.
4. Ron Currie, *God Is Dead* (Picador, 2007).
5. The translation in the footnote gives a better rendering of this verse than the main text.
6. Lesslie Newbigin, *The Open Secret* (Eerdmans, 1978), p. 36.
7. C. S. Lewis, *Miracles* (William Collins, 2012), p. 178.
8. Matthew Parris, 'Calm down! He's not President of the World', *The Times*, 8 November 2010.
9. See *Metro* newspaper, 8 April 2013.
10. John Stott, *Basic Christianity* (IVP, 2002), p. 21.

Chapter 2 Christianity is 100% critical

1. Francis Schaeffer, *The Great Evangelical Disaster* (Crossway, 1984), p. 23.
2. Alexander Solzhenitsyn, *The Gulag Archipelago 1918–1956*, vol. 1 (Westview Press, 1998), p. 168.
3. Julian Barnes, *Nothing to Be Frightened Of* (Vintage, 2009), p. 1.

Chapter 3 Christianity is 100% credible

1. Richard Dawkins, *The God Delusion* (Bantam Press, 2006), p. 37.
2. For example, see N. T. Wright, *Justification: God's Plan and Paul's Vision* (SPCK, 2009).
3. The italics in both quotations are mine.
4. Dawkins, *God Delusion*, p. 23.
5. Richard Dawkins, interview with Justin Brierly, 21 August 2013: www.youtube.com/watch?v=NZ6t7Lqrdvc – see 9m 25s into clip.

Part 2 100% passion

1. John Piper, *When I Don't Desire God: How to Fight for Joy* (Crossway, 2004), p. 31.
2. Jonathan Edwards, *Religious Affections* (1746).

Chapter 4 Christianity is 100% struggle

1. I am grateful to Ian Garrett for this illustration; Jesmond Parish Church, 7 March 1999.
2. D. Martyn Lloyd-Jones, *The Christian Soldier* (Baker, 1998).
3. This idea is adapted from St Helen's Bishopsgate's 'Read Mark Learn' commentary on Romans, pp. 66–68.
4. If you struggle with pornography, two great resources that can help are the website www.covenanteyes.com and Tim Chester's book, *Captured by a Better Vision* (IVP, 2010).

Chapter 5 Christianity is 100% Spirit-empowered

1. J. I. Packer, *Keeping in Step with the Spirit*, 2nd edn (Baker, 2005), p. 57.

2. Gordon Fee, *Paul, the Spirit and the People of God* (Baker Academic, 1996), p. 180.

3. John Stott, *The Message of Romans: God's Good News for the World*, The Bible Speaks Today (IVP, 1994), p. 225.

4. Profiles: Michael Aspel, 'I'm just not a happy person', *Independent*, 25 May 2004.

5. Irenaeus, *Against Heresies*, 4.20.7.

6. J. I. Packer, *Knowing God* (Hodder and Stoughton, 2005), p. 232. Italics in orginal by Packer.

7. Galatians 4:1–7 makes the same point. The sending of the Son enables our status as God's children, but it is the sending of the Spirit which enables our experience of being God's children.

8. Graham Beynon, *Experiencing the Spirit: New Testament Essentials for Every Christian* (IVP, 2010), p. 46.

9. Russell Moore, *Adopted for Life: The Priority of Adoption for Christian Families and Churches* (Crossway, 2009), p. 52.

10. Ibid., p. 25.

11. Ibid., p. 52.

12. I was first alerted to Russell Moore's book and the link to our adoption into God's family by a fantastic talk I heard by Tim Chester.

13. See www.youtube.com/watch?v=A440EcmDn1c.

14. Fee, *Paul, the Spirit and the People of God*, p. 180.

Chapter 6 Christianity is 100% satisfaction

1. 'Believe TV channel "exploited viewers" says Ofcom', *Independent*, 22 August 2011.

2. Victor Hugo, *Les Misérables*, vol. 1 (Wordsworth, 1994), p. 112.

3. With thanks to Jonathan Fletcher for this illustration.

4. John Owen, *The Mortification of Sin*, ch. 13, using Zechariah 12:10.

5. This concept of trusting in a good, gracious and great God was brought home to me very clearly and powerfully in a talk by Tim Chester in 2010, and these two paragraphs are a response to the content of that talk.

Part 3 100% life

1. Oonagh Blackman, 'My faith is private . . . it isn't relevant to my job', *Daily Mirror*, 20 January 2005.

2. Matthew Parris, 'Why Ruth Kelly's faith and her politics cannot be separated', *The Times*, 21 January 2005.

3. Nancy Pearcey, *Total Truth: Liberating Christianity from Its Cultural Captivity* (Crossway, 2008), p. 77.

4. Athanasius, *Life of Antony*, 85.

5. Benedict, quoted in Jonathan Hill, *The New Lion History of Christianity* (Lion Hudson, 2007), p. 221.

6. Mark Greene, *Supporting Christians at Work* (Administry and LICC, 2001), p. 6.

Chapter 7 Christianity is 100% inclusive

1. In John 3:10, Jesus' words to Nicodemus in the Greek are literally, 'You are *the* teacher of Israel.'

2. Thanks to Paul Williams for this illustration.

3. I first heard this illustration from Mark Ashton at St Andrew the Great, Cambridge.

Chapter 8 Christianity is 100% inter-relational

1. John Newton, quoted in Joseph F. Winks (ed.), *The Christian Pioneer* (1856), p. 84.

2. 'I want to be alone: The rise and rise of solo living', *Guardian*, 30 March 2012 (using Euromonitor data).

3. Thanks to Hugh Palmer for a helpful talk on Genesis 2 and to
   Tim Keller for a helpful talk on marriage that greatly helped
   me process these issues.
4. A very helpful website looking at the subject of
   homosexuality and same-sex attraction from a biblical and
   pastoral viewpoint is www.livingout.org.

Chapter 9 Christianity is 100% integrated

1. Some of the inspiration for using this marriage service phrase
   and some of the headings that follow come from Chris
   Wright's excellent book, *The Mission of God's People*
   (Zondervan, 2010), ch. 15.
2. Abraham Kuyper, 1800 Inaugural Lecture, Free University of
   Amsterdam.
3. Quoted in Timothy Keller, *Every Good Endeavour* (Hodder &
   Stoughton, 2012), p. 69.
4. John Stott notes these three motivations in his commentary:
   The Message of Romans: God's Good News for the World, The
   Bible Speaks Today (IVP, 1994), pp. 373–374.
5. David L. Edwards and John Stott, *Essentials: A Liberal–
   Evangelical Dialogue* (Hodder & Stoughton, 1988).
6. Preached in a sermon on my favourite verse of the Bible –
   1 Corinthians 10:31; John Venn, *Sermons*, vol. 2 (Nabu Press,
   2010), pp. 91–92.
7. Chris Wright (ed.), *John Stott: A Portrait by His Friends* (IVP,
   2011), p. 214.
8. William Hague, *William Wilberforce: The Life of the Great Anti-
   Slave Trade Campaigner* (Harper Perennial, 2008), p. 514.
9. Bernard of Clairvaux, *Selected Works*, trans. G. R. Evans
   (Paulist Press, 2000), p. 173.
10. Peter Scazzero, *The Emotionally Healthy Church: A Strategy for
    Discipleship that Actually Changes Lives* (Zondervan, 2010),
    pp. 206–207.

Conclusion: The case of the missing 'O'

1. William Wilberforce, *A Practical View of the Prevailing Religious System of Professed Christians in the Higher and Middle Classes in this Country, Contrasted with Real Christianity* (Dapper, 1797), (Kindle ebook: A Public Doman Book, Location 3883 of 4867).

For more information about IVP
and our publications visit
www.ivpbooks.com

Get regular updates at **ivpbooks.com/signup**
Find us on **facebook.com/ivpbooks**
Follow us on **twitter.com/ivpbookcentre**

Inter-Varsity Press, a company limited by guarantee registered in England and Wales, number 05202650. Registered office IVP Bookcentre, Norton Street, Nottingham NG7 3HR, United Kingdom. Registered charity number 1105757.